RELIGION
AND PRIME TIME
TELEVISION

RELIGION AND PRIME TIME TELEVISION

Edited by Michael Suman

Under the Auspices of the Center
for Communication Policy,
University of California, Los Angeles

 Westport, Connecticut
London

Library of Congress Cataloging-in-Publication Data

Religion and prime time television / edited by Michael Suman.
    p. cm.
    "Under the auspices of the Center for Communication Policy,
University of California, Los Angeles."
    Outgrowth of the Religion and Prime Time Television Conference,
held June 1, 1995, at the University of California, Los Angeles.
    Includes bibliographical references (p.) and index.
    ISBN 0-275-96034-X (alk. paper)
    1. Television broadcasting—United States—Religious aspects.
I. Suman, Michael, 1958- . II. UCLA Center for Communication
Policy. III. Religion and Prime Time Television Conference (1995 :
University of California, Los Angeles)
PN1992.6.R45 1997
261.5'2—dc21   97-19231

British Library Cataloguing in Publication Data is available.

Library of Congress Catalog Card Number: 97-19231
ISBN: 0-275-96034-X

First published in 1997

Praeger Publishers, 88 Post Road West, Westport, CT 06881
An imprint of Greenwood Publishing Group, Inc.

Printed in the United States of America

The paper used in this book complies with the
Permanent Paper Standard issued by the National
Information Standards Organization (Z39.48-1984).

10 9 8 7 6 5 4 3 2 1

Copyright Acknowledgments

The author and publisher gratefully acknowledge permission to use the following material:

Chapter 4, "God Taboo in Prime Time?" by Ellwood Kieser, originally appeared as "TV Finally Finds
Religion," in the *Los Angeles Times,* December 26, 1994, p. F3. Reprinted by permission of the
author.

Chapter 14, "Hollywood Makes Room for Religion" by Michael Medved, originally appeared in the
March/April 1995 issue of *The American Enterprise.* Reprinted with permission.

Contents

Acknowledgments

I wish to thank the following for their generous financial support that made the Religion and Prime Time Television Conference, which inspired this volume, possible: Cathy Siegel and The American Cinema Foundation, The Markle Foundation, The Nathan Cummings Foundation, David Horowitz and The Center for the Study of Popular Culture, The Lynde and Harry Bradley Foundation, The Scaife Family Foundation, and The Streisand Foundation.

Many thanks go to Marde Gregory, Jim Reynolds, Phoebe Schramm, and Scott Davis for their editorial assistance and general support. Scott Davis often provided invaluable computer assistance. Jim Reynolds provided many shrewd and useful editorial suggestions. I made countless trips to the office of Phoebe Schramm who always generously gave of her time when I asked for her sage advice on matters of wording and grammar. Marde Gregory made the initial contact with Greenwood to set up the publishing arrangement. She also provided frequent insightful editorial comments and did much of the work preparing the index.

Special thanks go to Gabriel Rossman for his tireless and enthusiastic work in helping me prepare and format the manuscript. Gabriel also did a lot of the work on the index. This marks the beginning of what I am sure will be a long and successful career for Gabriel in the world of publishing.

I would like to thank all of the contributors to this volume, each of whom has been cooperative in adding his or her unique voice.

And lastly, I would like to thank Jeff Cole, Director of the Center for Communication Policy, for his ideas, support, and the opportunity of putting this volume together.

Introduction

This book is an outgrowth of the Religion and Prime Time Television Conference that the UCLA Center for Communication Policy, along with the American Cinema Foundation and the Center for the Study of Popular Culture, hosted on June 1, 1995. This book is both a manifestation and a continuation of the debate that occurred at that conference.

Our ultimate goal at the UCLA Center is to have concrete, practical effects on how the mass media actually operate. With this in mind, we periodically host conferences focusing on controversial issues pertaining to the mass media. Our aim is to bring together leading figures from the worlds of academia, the media industry, and other relevant groups and organizations to meet and discuss the issue at hand. The first such conference we hosted was the Information Superhighway Summit which featured Vice President Albert Gore, FCC Chairman Reed Hundt, and the chief executive officers of practically every major film studio and communications technology company in America. At the June 1995 conference our topic was how religion is portrayed on prime time fiction television and the effect this has on our society.

A select group of participants from this conference was chosen to make contributions to this book. Their articles focus on the most important messages they believe need to be heard on the issue of religion on prime time fiction television. The writers, all national figures prominent in their respective fields, are a varied lot and provide a great diversity of viewpoints on the issue.

The book is divided into five parts. The first part includes key speeches delivered at the conference by religious figures. Donald Wildmon, the Christian leader of the American Family Association, argues that religion is rarely portrayed on television and, when it is, it is usually presented as a negative and destructive force. In watching television, viewers get the message that religion hardly exists in American society and, when it does, it is not a good thing. He asserts that the television industry is controlled by areligious people and it corrupts America's values. John Patrick Foley of the Vatican spoke on the ideal treatment of religion on prime time television. He asserts that the best treatment of religion and religious themes to date occurred on "The Waltons." This show realistically portrayed religious faith and how it contributes to the formation of people of integrity and idealism. He laments that such a show is so rare. Joan Brown Campbell, head of the National Council of Churches, argues for the need for greater dialogue between the two greatest storytellers of our culture—television and organized religion. She outlines areas in which the religious community and the media industry can work together so that television builds rather than erodes the common good.

Part II is composed of contributions from religious leaders. Ellwood Kieser, a Catholic priest who heads the organization behind the Humanitas Award, argues that television, in ignoring religion, has shied away from that part of us which is most essentially human. Television acts as if the human soul does not exist. If religion is so important, why isn't it reflected in television entertainment? Why is God taboo in prime time? Kieser reviews possible reasons for this. He also believes the situation is starting to change because of the realization that the search for God is the great drama of every human life. Dan Barker, an atheist leader from the Freedom From Religion Foundation, argues that the nonreligious constitute a significant segment of the population, and that we must remember this when arguing how television should accurately reflect American life. He offers as suggestions for television programming stories depicting nonbelievers and their dramatic lives. He also laments that television reflects the general American assumption that it's not nice to be critical of religion, an impulse he would rather encourage. A. James Rudin, a rabbi affiliated with the American Jewish Committee, argues that it's time to end the contentious relationship that exists between religion and prime time television. The television industry is hesitant to include religious characters because they don't want to offend anyone. Since clergy can't be shown as flawed in any way, they are limited to portrayals involving hatching, matching, and dispatching people. He maintains that there is need for an ongoing program of consultation and cooperation between the religious and television communities. Havanpola Ratanasara, executive president of the American Buddhist Congress, offers a Buddhist perspective on television programming. He outlines the religious and ethical responsibilities involved in programming decisions, and the consequences those decisions have both for the individuals making them and the wider society.

The third part of the book includes articles from the academic community. Margaret Miles, a theologian at the University of California at Berkeley, explains how complaints that religion is underrepresented and is usually portrayed as negative or dangerous don't adequately attend to the crucial issues surrounding media representations of religion. Miles argues that religion should be depicted as part of characters' everyday lives and that television will serve America well if it seeks to represent American religion as diverse, complex, and in need of critical examination. Judith Buddenbaum, a professor of technical journalism at Colorado State

University, presents the results of a survey of leaders of sixty-five American churches. The leaders complain that television does not portray religion well, ignores and denigrates religion, undermines cherished values and behaviors, and is actually responsible for a decrease in religiosity and an increase in criminal and immoral behavior. Buddenbaum points out notable differences in the responses of leaders from different traditions and takes issue with some of their fears. She stresses that the different religious groups must be sensitive to the pluralistic nature of American society and open to attacks, criticisms, and portrayals they find offensive if their own freedoms of belief and expression are to be protected. Wade Clark Roof, a sociologist and professor of religion and society at the University of California, Santa Barbara, writes on the blurring of boundaries between religion and the media. He explains how television has transformed religious discourse by softening it and making it less offensive. Television has also injected religious interpretations with current cultural categories, particularly those emphasizing the self. Religions, tamed by television, come to look more like one another, and religious faith merely becomes another of television's "symbolic repertoires," little different from other reward-promising representations. Another blurred boundary relates to when religious meanings and values find expression in secular programming. In this regard television presents a fluid sense of self, encouraging individuals, less rooted in tradition, to pick and choose among religious and spiritual themes. But television also presents existential encounters which can provoke religious and spiritual responses and assumes some of the functions traditionally ascribed to religious myth and ritual. Michael Suman, a sociologist at UCLA and editor of this volume, asks, "Do we really need more religion on prime time fiction TV?" He doubts that we do. He fears that it will only lead to further incidents of religious bigotry, harassment, and intolerance, of which we have already had far too much in our history. He offers a historical overview of such intolerance and argues that, in light of this, the United States has wisely limited the extent to which religion has entered the public square. He fears the motives and intentions of the religious right, who, he argues, is behind most of the present criticism. Jack Shaheen, a professor emeritus in mass communications at Southern Illinois University, explains how Muslims are ignored on prime time television and, when portrayed, are depicted negatively and stereotypically caricaturized.

Part IV is composed of articles written by media critics and journalists. Thomas Plate, a columnist for the *Los Angeles Times*, argues that "the only thing worse for America than religious topics not dealt with on prime time TV would be religious topics dealt with during prime time." He insists that television is not suited for handling spiritual matters or dealing with the diversity of American religious life. Michael Medved, chief film critic for the *New York Post*, discusses the rediscovery of traditional Christianity and Judaism by the television and film community. He argues that although there are certainly still negative characterizations of religious folk and the profit motive is still more important than the prophet motive, more balanced portrayals and pro-faith messages are evident and there is less religion bashing. Ted Baehr, chairman of the Christian Film and Television Commission, argues that religion is alive and well on network prime time fiction television, but that the religion portrayed is not Christianity. Instead, we see a cacophony of other religions, such as materialism, consumerism, eroticism, humanism, and the cult of violence. Many Christian believers feel alienated from the culture they witness on television, a culture which lacks characters with a religious faith like their own and which emphasizes values which are at odds with their own.

The fifth part includes articles written by representatives of the television industry. Lionel Chetwynd, a writer, director, and producer, argues that the television industry avoids religion because it doesn't want to risk controversy. Television, in fact, shies away from dealing with the issues of the day in general, although this has not always been the case. Chetwynd relates this change to the fracturing of the common culture of America, a 1960s change in the conventional wisdom that ethical values are most importantly transferred by religion, and a change from a notion of balanced programming to one of "balance within programming." Chetwynd argues that religion will only return to mass broadcasting when the nation restores a civil public dialogue. Bob Gale, another writer, director, and producer, discusses the historical and cultural reasons why the most religious and devout in society are those least likely to end up in show business. He also offers both the dramatist's and the business answer as to why there are so few religious characters on television and why the church as an institution is so seldom seen. Danny Goldberg, a record company executive, takes exception to some of the criticisms leveled by religious figures against the entertainment industry. He stresses that television entertainment is driven by entertainment values, not religious ones, and only rarely can a work of entertainment satisfy an audience in terms of entertainment value and carry a religious message. For the most part, television is a business which must attract millions to satisfy advertisers, and it is a rare talent who can produce spiritually uplifting entertainment that can be successful on television as it exists. We must also keep in mind that there are many interest groups tugging at television from many different directions, and that too much of this pressure creates a siege mentality. And this type of mindset only fosters mediocrity, conformity to the status quo, and lack of creativity, making it all the harder to adequately and accurately portray true religious experience.

In an addendum Gabriel Rossman, an aspiring sociologist, directly responds to Don Wildmon's essay, which opens this collection. Rossman argues that one program which was singled out as negative toward religion is actually a positive depiction and that such unfair accusations are responsible for scaring the media away from featuring religion in prime time television.

In sum, what this book offers is the wide-ranging viewpoints of a select group of individuals, drawn from the religious, journalistic, academic, and television industry communities, on the important public policy debate surrounding this issue.

As this book comes to print in 1997, an increased number of shows featuring religion have winged their way onto television, following on the success of the CBS hit "Touched by an Angel." The 1996-97 season featured WB's "7th Heaven" and CBS's "Promised Land." These were joined by ABC's "Soul Man" as a mid-season replacement. The 1997-98 season will bring "Nothing Sacred" and "Teen Angel" to ABC and "Good News" to UPN.

This modest change in the television landscape will no doubt be greeted with excitement by some and dismay by others. Regardless, the fundamental issues as discussed by the contributors to this book remain fundamentally the same. The debate will be ongoing. This book is offered as a constructive beginning.

I

Conference Speeches by
Religious Figures

It Is Time to End Religious Bigotry

Donald E. Wildmon

Once, while traveling in Europe, our guide asked me my profession. I told her that I was a minister. She then asked me what branch of government I worked in. The concept of an American minister being a clergyman never entered her mind.

At first, I wondered why she thought American ministers worked for the government. Then I recalled that many European governments have *ministers* of education, of interior, et cetera. Has she been to America? No. Where then did she get her perception of America? It came from watching American television programs.

Watching those programs, she did not learn that America is—at its core—a religious country. Her view should not be too surprising. Even we Americans who watch television reach the same conclusion.

Watching TV, one quickly comes to the conclusion that sports are more popular than religion. On TV hardly anyone ever attends church, or prays, or seriously discusses religion. On TV religion hardly exists in American society. And when it does, it is far more often presented as a destructive force rather than a constructive force.

The late AP religion writer George Cornell wrote a column about religion and sports shortly before he died. He did research and found that the amount of money contributed to religion in 1992 totaled $56.7 billion. That is about 14 times the $4 billion spent on the three biggest sports—major league baseball, football, and basketball.

In attendance, religion totaled 5.6 billion in 1993, based on annual Gallup Polls. That is about 55 times greater than the 103 million total attendance reported by the three main professional sports leagues.

The latest tally of overall attendance at all U.S. sporting events, gathered in 1990 by the *Daily Racing Form*, totaled 388 million including both professional and college football, baseball, basketball, and hockey, and also boxing, tennis, soccer, wrestling, and harness, automobile, and dog racing.

In comparison, in 1990, the total religious attendance was 5.2 billion, almost 13 times greater than that of all sporting events combined. The total attendance for worship in just one month—about 430 million—was greater than the 388 million total for the whole year at all sporting events.

Why this misperception on television about the centrality of religion in the social fabric of America? Lee Rich, Hollywood producer, gave the answer to that question during a debate I had with him years ago. "I haven't been to church in twenty years," Mr. Rich said, "and I don't know anyone else who goes to church." Mr. Rich's comment was confirmed by the Lichter/Rothman study showing that of the media elite responsible for our entertainment programs, 93% say they seldom or never attend religious services while 45% claim no religion at all.

Columnist Mona Charen recently reported on one study which showed that in more than 1,000 hours of entertainment reviewed by the Media Research Center, negative references to the clergy outnumbered positive ones 4-to-1. Portrayals of lay believers were even worse, with 68% of churchgoers depicted negatively and only 18% shown positively.

More obvious than the negative presentation of people of faith, however, is the censorship of religion from prime time television. The Media Research Center reported that of 1,716 hours of original programming on the four largest networks last year, there were only 253 portrayals of religion. The message from TV is quite clear—religion hardly exists in American society and when it does it is not a good thing.

Even more telling about Hollywood's attitude toward religion is its treatment of values. Values are a by-product of one's religion. When two-thirds of those entertainment media elite told Lichter/Rothman that they wanted to use their programming to reshape American society, they weren't kidding—and they knew who and what they had in mind.

On a recent "Law & Order" episode, a band of self-righteous, murdering pro-lifers led by an ex-priest, were contrasted against a caring and courageous abortionist. On Fox's "House of Buggin'," three women in a singing group discuss their sexual preferences—bondage, the kind of men they like, et cetera. Before they go on stage, one prays that God will make her a lesbian so she can love her singing partners. Another thanks God for a defective condom that allowed her to get pregnant. And they go on stage to sing about fornication, late periods, and emasculating men. All of this, of course, is accompanied by canned laughter.

On CBS's "The Five Mrs. Buchanans," the dense and ditzy blonde former stripper, now married to a preacher, sings "O Little Gown of Bethlehem." She hasn't a clue as to why believers celebrate Christmas, saying, "I just love Christmas—a time that we set aside to remember what's good and decent in all of us."

A sister-in-law, excited about the city's house decorating contest, vows, "Mrs. O'Leary's head is gonna be spinning when I rip that blue ribbon out of her greedy little Catholic hand!" And their Jewish sister-in-law observes: "You Christians really have this holiday spirit down, don't you!"

ABC decided that one episode of "Roseanne" was so good that the network aired it not just once, or even twice, but three times. Dan and Roseanne discover that D.J. has been lying about where he spends his afternoons. They assign Darlene to follow him. She reports, "[I]t's worse than you thought. He's going to church!"

When D.J. confirms Darlene's report, Roseanne insists that D.J. can ask them anything he wants to know about God.

"What religion are we?" asks D.J.

"I have no idea," mom snarls.

Roseanne answers a phone call and arranges for the caller to see a new stove for sale at her diner. She says she won it in a game show. The truth was that a company mistakenly delivered two stoves instead of one.

D.J. confronts his mom: "You were never on any game show."

"I was too on a game show. And if you didn't spend all your time down at that da-- church, you'd know that!" mom screams back.

Later, D.J. asks why Roseanne makes him lie about his age when they go to the movies. "[M]ore money to give to charity," she lies.

Finally, D.J. declares, "I don't think Darlene and David should be having sex without being married." Roseanne and Dan both refuse to address the issue. Darlene changes the subject by suggesting D.J. ask mom about the stove she's stealing. Roseanne insists that the company "gave" it to her, and that it's nothing to the "big company" which "screws little people" like her all the time.

Roseanne sells the stove and divides the money with her partners. Confronted by D.J. even as they divide the spoils, Roseanne screams at her child, "Get off my back!! Even God took a day off!!"

Simply put, the story is that of a young boy searching for a moral anchor. He raises the issues of lying, cheating, stealing, and illicit teen sex, and on every point his family ridicules, patronizes, or openly attacks him for implying that there aren't any standards of right and wrong in his family. Such is the state of prime time TV.

About fifteen years ago, in Aspen, Colorado, I sat across a room from Steven Bochco (currently producer of "NYPD Blue"). He was one of about fifty producers and advertisers who were meeting with me and one other concerned activist discussing the impact of television on our society. I remember little else about that meeting except this: Mr. Bochco said he was going to push the limits of television as far as he could. He did not say that he was going to produce the most entertaining, beneficial, helpful programs that would contribute to a more moral and productive society. Rather his ambition was to push the limits of television as far as he could. I must confess that Mr. Bochco's attitude tends to be the norm, rather than the exception, in Hollywood.

When 88% of all sexual activity portrayed on TV occurs between people not married to each other, television makes lust more attractive than love. When children see 100,000 acts of violence by the time they graduate from high school, television has helped produce the impression that violence is a normal experience in life, and by implication that it is acceptable behavior.

The responsibility for the current treatment of religion and religious values on

TV must be jointly shared by the TV industry and those in organized religious communities, who by their silence have condoned this practice.

By including a realistic presentation of religion and religious values in its programming, television could help make ours a less violent and a more moral and stable society.

What do people of faith expect from prime time television? Just fair play, that's all.

Why Not More Programs Like "The Waltons"?

John Patrick Foley

I have been asked—what do I think would be the ideal treatment of religion in prime time television?

I would have to say that the best treatment of religion and of religious themes that I can remember on television was done in that wonderful series "The Waltons."

There, faith and religion were integrated into the story of a normal yet exceptional family which had its struggles and its trials, its moments of joy and satisfaction—but almost always in a context of faith and of dependence upon God. That treatment did not mean that there were not also trials of faith itself for some members of the family; that treatment did not mean that members of the clergy were always portrayed as saints. That treatment did mean that religion mattered and was a factor in the lives of the Waltons—and it was evident that it touched their lives deeply. They were not afraid to talk about God—even to question Him occasionally. And they were not afraid to talk about the meaning of suffering, about death, and about eternal life.

It was important that the Waltons didn't preach; they lived and experienced their faith. They sometimes had difficulties with it, but they believed, and in that belief they found strength, consolation, and courage. In the midst of recurring poverty and occasional pain, they lived with dignity, mutual respect, love, and fundamental happiness because they recognized that their existence and their dignity came from God.

I must confess that I often cried when I watched the Waltons—because the series often touched me deeply. Perhaps I identified with John-Boy, because I too tried to be a writer when I was a boy and a young man. Perhaps I recalled the example of prayer and faith of my own parents, not expressed in showy pietism, but in a spirit of profound conviction, of integrity, of prayerfulness. Perhaps I saw in the grandparents my own grandparents and in the friends and relatives of the

Waltons my own friends and relatives.

It was important for me as a viewer and as a person of faith to see that religion was not treated superficially, unrealistically, as something ridiculous, or as merely an institution. It was treated as a conviction about the meaning of life and about the dignity and destiny of the human person and about our radical dependence upon a loving, but often mysterious, God.

The Waltons were Protestants, Appalachian Protestants, who are often treated by the media as obscurantist rednecks. This was not the treatment religion or middle-American Protestantism received in "The Waltons." The Waltons and their faith were treated with understanding, comprehension, and respect—and we, as Americans who come from perhaps the most religious nation on earth and whose national motto is "One Nation Under God," identified with the program in a way we do not identify with flippant situation comedies which mock religion or with depictions of clergy or of nuns as caricatures or with manipulation of religion as possibly superstitious or at least quaint.

The Waltons were believable people with a believable faith—and we watched them and identified with them and even cried with them, because we gained an insight into ourselves, into our purpose, and into our dignity and destiny. We realized in watching the Waltons that it is not what we have that makes us great, but what we are; we watched members of the Walton family learn that lesson. We learned respect for the sick, appreciation for the elderly, and patience with those experiencing the pangs of growth. We learned how to live in the presence of God with the realization that we will one day have to answer to Him as a loving but exigent judge.

What would be the ideal treatment of religion on prime time television? In so many ways, I think we've already seen it in "The Waltons"—the realism and the authenticity of real religious faith—and the contribution of that faith in the formation of men and women of integrity and of idealism.

I have seen with what sensitivity television in prime time can treat religious faith; and I am only disappointed that it does it so seldom.

Tuning In to Common Concerns: An Invitation from the Churches to the Media Industry

Joan Brown Campbell

What does a couch potato have in common with a worshipper in the pew? More than you might think! Both listen to compelling stories. Both are shaped by what they hear from the two most powerful storytellers in our culture: television and organized religion.

If you get right down to it, we are really talking about the same person in different settings, as the huge audiences for soaps, sitcoms, and sermons pretty much overlap. The storytellers, however, have yet to open a sustained dialogue with each other, despite the great potential benefits. Those who preach sermons and run Sunday school classes need to know the implications, for example, of the fact that television plays for an average of seven hours a day in American households. Those who write the series and produce news programs need to know that they are speaking to a people who display a higher degree of religiosity than any other nation in the industrialized world.

THE POWER OF STORIES

Television and religion both speak to an audience as hungry for stories as our tribal ancestors, who sat around campfires eager for a retelling of the myths and legends that bound them together. At its best, television offers stories worth telling because they enhance values that build community. At worst, viewers absorb stories of random violence and amorality that increase their fear of other people and thus further divide our communities.

Speaking as the General Secretary of the National Council of Churches, I would point out that Christians, too, have their stories, starting with the life of Christ, who himself was a gifted teller of parables, the wonderful teaching stories. From the very beginning, we knew that the way to talk to people was, in fact, in stories, and that the most popular tales are all about our fellow human beings.

Storytellers almost always tell tales about human characters. We know from experience, and from what researchers have discovered about the evolution of humans as social beings, that people learn the most profound lessons from watching and hearing other people and that we have an insatiable appetite for information about other people.

So to the degree that television, and the church, for that matter, focuses on the lives of individuals, the audience is, in turn, informed, inspired, horrified, and shocked, but always interested. In negative form, these stories are gossip and they have sold well since time began. No doubt the element of gossip accounts for the success of some tabloid-style programs and for "reality based" programs that show our neighbors at the worst moments of their lives.

The Bible makes a point of saying that we should be very careful about how we speak of one another, that we shall not bear false witness against each other. Programming that perpetuates the most destructive "gossip" in our society by consistently portraying black men as criminals, women as victims, and vengeance seekers as heroes falls into that category. So do exploitative talk shows that seem to assert that lurid and bizarre behavior has become the norm among our neighbors.

The more realistic such programming appears, the more devastating it can be. Let me propose just one alternative idea, just as a discussion starter. Why not create a "911 format" about ministers, priests, and rabbis? Along with police, firefighters, and medical personnel, who is called on more frequently in times of emergency than the clergy? It might be a real draw for the public to see how the leaders of churches respond to the thousands of emergencies that pull them into action day after day. Just an idea.

OUR APPROACH TO MEDIA

Religious bodies take the media very seriously. Since its beginning in 1950, the National Council of Churches has maintained a dialogue with the media industry on the issue of ethics in communication—concentrating on film in the early years but quickly branching out into the areas of broadcasting and then cable and other technologies. While others attempted to mold the media through tactics such as boycotts, we honored good films with awards, maintained a Hollywood office, encouraged broadcasters to meet community programming needs, held hearings on media violence in which industry representatives participated, and much more.

Recently we updated our policy statement on violence in the media, which calls for all sectors of society, including the media industry, to share the responsibility for finding remedies. The policy aims at involving many people in voluntary actions that will preempt a call for government censorship. In our statement, we acknowledge that "We Christians support the media industry as consumers thereby helping to form their financial backbone. We are indeed part of the audience that media violence attracts." It is important to make this confessional statement. We are part of the problem as well as part of the solution. We permit, and sometimes encourage, our children's exposure to media with violent content. We participate in the media industries through our investments and through our vocations as producers and writers. We do not always use the power that is ours to work for better programming, and at times, we must confess, we shirk our duty as citizens to be vigilant in the pursuit of a common good.

Just as we have engaged the media in a serious and thoughtful way, we expect that the media should also take the churches seriously. Just for starters, there are the sheer numbers to consider. In the National Council of Churches alone, which encompasses 33 of the more than 200 denominations in the United States, we are 51 million people in more than 140,000 congregations. My daughter, who is a politician in the state of Ohio, once said to me, "Mother, no one has more bases in the neighborhoods of the nation than churches, except perhaps bars and schools." I have often pondered that image. Along with synagogues and mosques, churches are a strong and powerful force, politically, socially, and as a teacher of religious and cultural values.

If the churches and the television industry deepen the conversation that we have had, I believe we would discover paths to cooperation that have seldom been explored. We already have hints as to where these could lead. I think, for example, of executive producer Ken Wales, whose credits include "Christy," a CBS series that Ken says features "stories of love and honor and loyalty and, yes, sacrifice." Churches across the country agreed and have embraced this program. Recently, Ken showed me a study guide for "Christy" in brochure form. Here is a way in which religious organizations and congregations can study and reinforce positive television programming. The opportunity is great. I can say from experience that congregations everywhere are looking for high-quality material for adult study groups.

Perhaps some in the television industry fear to tread in this direction, wary of getting involved in sectarian disputes, or of being accused of using the public airwaves to promote a particular religious belief. They are acutely aware that their audiences are religiously diverse. I would reply that the members of the National Council of Churches have demonstrated a spirit of ecumenical and interfaith cooperation in the programming they produce for network television and for the Faith & Values Channel, which involves a wide variety of faith groups. Further, in the early formative stages of Faith & Values, the National Council of Churches was among participants who pushed for standards to insure that no programming by Faith & Values members would defame other religious groups. Our Christian faith, like the beliefs of most religious groups, inspires us to promote the common good. I think that it is this press toward what Martin Luther King, Jr., called the "beloved community" that most unites the diverse religious groups of this nation.

TELEVISION AND THE COMMON GOOD

Speaking in testimony to the United States Congress, the National Council of Churches said this about the common good: "It is the delicate and precious part of life that needs our voice. It is the social contract that is always attacked and threatened by the excessively private. It is our life together that needs our earnest advocacy. It has always been the religious mandate, when it has found its best voice, to speak for the well-being of all. Who else will speak for the whole family and its well-being if other voices are privatized and self-serving? It has always been the religious insight that self-interest, greed, and self-aggrandizement need no advocate; they can be counted on to defend and serve themselves."

Now, television can greatly affect the common good. It can erode the common good, and it can build the common good. Television can, for example, reinforce materialism. It can, and often does, increase a kind of greed and individualism that disrupts all efforts toward building community. Further, I think our self-centeredness and our materialism is at the very root of the violence we see in our society. An unhealthy preoccupation with acquiring and protecting material things, and the accompanying devaluation of our relationships with fellow human beings, sets the stage for all kinds of violence. Therefore, we must be as concerned about this destructive attitude as we are about the actual violence that we see on television.

I have a deep concern as well about the creation of dangerous polarities in our communities that I think television often exacerbates. I have heard it said that producers of programs are being pressed to seek balance. I would argue with that. Programs often "balance" the views of the radical left with those of the radical right and feel that fairness and the common good have been served. Have they? A show that brings representatives of the right and the left into confrontation undoubtedly creates dramatic television. It also creates the impression there is no broad center, that there is no common goal. This is necessary, we are told, because conflict is news. We are told that it is balanced, because views on both extremes are carried. I wish we could search together for a balance that reinforces the fact that there is indeed a very broad center and many people who live within it. If we focused there, those who are the most radical would be pushed to the sparsely populated edges where, in fact, they belong.

Television also is important to our common life because it can create leaders, stars, and heroes. And it can destroy them. I worry about that. From my own experience, I know that one minute on "Today" generates more mail than I can handle. And I well remember that more than a decade ago, the National Council of Churches and its member communions spent two years defending themselves after the airing of an ill-conceived and inaccurate segment on the show "60 Minutes." We are more than aware that an appearance on prime time can build or destroy in a blink of the eye.

Of course, we need heroes. But people in the television industry must be very mindful of what it means to create and break down leadership. There are religious leaders who are accountable to a structure and to a body of believers and who in fact are charged with providing spiritual leadership. There are also any number of spokespersons for what we call the "religious right," for lack of a better term. Some among them constitute a cultural phenomenon and have received enormous media attention. They may well be news and thus deserve coverage, but it would be inaccurate to portray them as religious leaders.

Genuine religious teachings always draw adherents into an ever-widening circle of understanding, respect, and compassion. To the extent that television reinforces movement in this direction by making us aware of our neighbors' joys and struggles, television performs a great service. It is certainly true that hearts and wallets open when people see the suffering caused by disastrous events that may occur half-a-world away. Television can expand the generosity that has always been a mark of the American people. But television may also be changing the very way we perceive and experience traumatic world events. Let me tell you a true story. When the Los Angeles riots of 1992 began, I was awakened at four o'clock in the morning with a call from the head of the Council of Churches in South Korea. He was very upset. I had not been awake at that hour, but, in a different time zone, he had already seen the riots on CNN, and he wanted me to do something about the portrayal of Koreans on that channel. And so, while television does open the world to us, it may also alter the way we respond to that world. I was certainly challenged to take into account the reality of viewers far removed from me by culture and geography, yet closely linked in many other ways.

Television also can expose evil and raise moral and ethical questions to new levels in the national consciousness, as it did, for example, in the aftermath of the Oklahoma City bombing. Did we as a nation pay any attention to the existence of militia groups? Not until they were exposed on television. What if this great power to affect public perception was used to rectify the inaccurate and negative public images of those who are affected by racism, by sexism, and by poverty? What would happen if television portrayed poor people in all their humanity, not as statistics and stereotypes? My guess is the entire welfare debate would change if we could begin to understand all of the poor people in this country who live in the best possible way that they can with extremely limited resources.

Our churches know these stories because they are close to the community. African American churches, for example, carry out extraordinary ministries in poor urban neighborhoods, as well as in more affluent settings. They are part of the great religious and cultural mix, the diversity in unity, that is the National Council. In addition to six historic African American churches, the National Council of Churches includes "peace churches" such as Quaker meetings, the mainline Protestant churches, a denomination made up largely of Korean-Americans and new Korean immigrants, and nine Orthodox churches that have ethnic roots in Greece, Syria, Russia, the Ukraine, and other places where Eastern and Oriental Orthodoxy have long histories.

Given the organization I represent, I cannot leave the subject of religion and television without saying a word about the importance of religious freedom. In my work, I have observed the struggle for religious liberty in many countries on every continent, and I have concluded that, comparatively speaking, Americans fail to value this freedom. Perhaps it is the inevitable result of living for so many generations under a system that has guaranteed religious freedom. We hardly give it a thought.

But we are living in times when intolerance is being voiced in new and disturbing ways. And so, even as we work toward a better portrayal, a fairer portrayal, and perhaps a more intentional portrayal of religion and values in television, we must do so in ways that respect people of all beliefs or of no beliefs in this pluralistic nation of ours. Roger Williams, who founded the colony of Rhode Island as a haven of religious liberty over three hundred years ago, left vivid reminders in his writings of the lived truth about religious freedom. To paraphrase Williams, coerced religion, on its good days, produces hypocrites, and on its bad days, it produces rivers of blood. In these days of religious strife in so many countries, we would do well to reaffirm the roots of our own religious freedom and to preserve a system in which the state secures peace and stability, but never aspires to holiness. Only in this way can we maintain liberty and justice for all.

OUR INVITATION

I have suggested a brief outline of areas in which the churches and the media industry could work toward the common good. Now I would like to suggest the kind of expertise that churches bring to such a partnership. Religion in America, indeed in the world, is complex, nuanced, and frequently fraught with difficult or even troubling ambiguities. There is a lot more to know about it than you can get from those easy-to-find people who believe they are experts in religion because they belong to a congregation, know some hymns, and can quote the Scriptures. Their well-meaning attitude ignores the breadth and diversity of the religious community, as well as the intricacies of its beliefs and structures, and can produce simplistic rather than simple answers to questions that often require more than easy or glib answers.

Call on experts in the religious community whenever you need some facts or some interpretation on an issue large or small. There may be people in your own backyard, so to speak, who can provide important information and illuminating insights because their religious faith and service have brought them close to particular issues or events. They also may be able to make more comprehensible the answers to difficult questions about moral and ethical choices.

But the more far-reaching suggestion I want to make is this: I hope that the leaders of the media industry, however you define them, might meet once a year, or even twice a year, with a panel representing the broad spectrum of religious leadership. I believe that Roman Catholic leaders, prominent Jewish rabbis, and leaders of other faiths would join me in this suggestion. I believe that religious leadership cares deeply about the media. We quarrel with you at times and you quarrel with us at times, but we each understand the other's power.

The very top leadership in the religious community in this country would make themselves available to you because you need expertise in the field of religion, just as you need it in foreign affairs, just as you need it in other fields. And the religious community—with its wide spectrum of beliefs, practices, and understandings, its broad center and rambunctious fringes—needs to speak with you. Together we need to talk about a goal to which I honestly believe we are all committed. And that great goal is a nonviolent society that makes way for the common good, that builds the beloved community.

II
Articles by
Religious Leaders

God Taboo in Prime Time?

Ellwood E. Kieser

From the pilgrims to the present, religion has always been an important part of American life. Throughout our history, most Americans have made religious faith a crucial ingredient in their search for fulfillment; they have tried to root their lives in a transcendent ground. When it worked, religious faith enabled them to tap into a source of energy that empowered them to take charge of their lives and exercise their freedom in a responsible way. It supplied meaning in their lives, helped them discover who they are, choose the values by which they would live, and reach out in love to their fellow human beings.

This may explain why 94% of the American people say they believe in God, why 41% attend a church or synagogue on any given weekend, why religious books are perennials on the bestseller lists.

Yet, if religion is central to American culture, it has been curiously absent from broadcast television in the United States. It is not that commercial television has attacked the spiritual dimension of the human personality. It has done what is much worse. It has ignored this most important part of the human psyche.

In doing so, it has shied away from that part of us which is most essentially human, that intimate place where we talk to ourselves and to all those other people who live within us. This is where we do all kinds of important things: fantasize, intuit, create, make commitments, grapple with mystery, struggle for meaning, perceive the sacred, respond to the holy, feel awe and wonder, reach for that which is above and beyond ourselves, and enter into communion with the ground of our being.

Freud called this portion of the human personality the unconscious because it is shrouded in mystery and can neither be weighed nor measured. The Greeks called it soul because it is preeminently spiritual. And the Bible calls it heart because it is where love resides and commitments are made.

Yet, for most of its history, American television has acted as if this part of us—let's call it the human soul—did not exist. "If religion is boring," asks Howard Rosenberg perceptively, "why is it important to so many people?" And if it is so important, why hasn't it been reflected in our televised entertainment? Why until recently had God been taboo in prime time?

Is it because, as some critics have maintained, the people of the entertainment community are more stridently secular, less godly than the rest of the community? (Could anyone who lives in this community and knows its people responsibly maintain that?)

Is it because the human soul and the God in whose image it is made are mysteries? We can grasp much about them. But we cannot grasp everything about them. Nor can we program them. Are they just too much for our boxed-in minds to handle?

Is it because many people, in the entertainment community as well as the viewing public, have confused God with their own superegos, pushing the tenderness and compassion of God into eclipse, leaving only a vindictive and fearsome tyrant that has nothing in common with the God of the Old and New Testaments?

Is it a feeling that entertainment is escapist and spiritual experience is concerned with the realest of the real and that the two, like oil and water, do not mix?

Is it a reluctance, born of spiritual sensitivity to take God's name in vain, to involve Him in the selling of soap?

There are no easy answers to these questions. But I do think there are now indications the old walls may be coming down. The times, they are a-changin'. Many contemporary series, especially those in the hour category, are delving into the hunger of their characters for spiritual connectedness and they are dramatizing their search for a transcendent ground and a spiritual center.

And they are discovering what Sophocles and Aeschylus, Shakespeare and George Bernard Shaw, Robert Bolt and Paddy Chayefsky learned before them: The search for God is the great drama of every human life; and because it is, stories that chronicle that search are intensely involving. They speak to us on some deep level and activate things inside of us that we did not know existed. Jeopardy, surprise, humor, high stakes, emotional accessibility—these stories have it all. Which is just another way of saying: There is nothing more exciting, more theatrical, than God.

Why? Because God is the loving mystery in whom we live and move and have our being. More than that, God is the beginning and the end, the meaning and the purpose, the ground and the horizon of all human life.

Unbelievers and Prime Time Television

Dan Barker

"If it's religious, it must be good." This pervasive idea in society is a mistake that we unbelievers feel is far too often mimicked on television.

Millions of good Americans do not believe in a god or the supernatural. According to the polls, between 5% and 9% of the people of the United States say they are atheists. *Christianity Today* reported one survey showing that 7.5% of Americans declare themselves to be godless. By comparison, Jews are a respected minority at 2% to 3%, or about one-third the size of atheists.

The National Survey of Religion and Politics (1992, University of Akron), showcased in the January 30, 1995, issue of *Time Magazine*, puts the "non-religious" at 18.5% of Americans, outnumbering mainline Protestants (18%) and surpassed only by Roman Catholics (23.4%) and Evangelicals (25.9%). *The 1995 Information Please Almanac* reports that the nonreligious and atheists are more than a billion (about 22%) worldwide.

Not only are we unbelievers a significant segment of the population, but those Americans who are religious are not as devout as they pretend. A study published in the December 1993 issue of *American Sociological Review* found that although roughly 40% of Americans regularly say they attend a place of worship on a weekly basis, only about half (19%) actually show up in the pews. (Church attendance is one of those factors of "social desirability" that are over-reported to pollsters.) This means that during any given non-holiday week, four out of five Americans do not attend church!

Freethinkers (atheists and agnostics) are a part of that "broad center" of American citizens who work hard, pay their taxes, do volunteer work, serve in the military, sit on juries, vote in elections, contribute to charity, work for political and social causes, and contribute to science, education, art, music, and literature. Some of them work in the entertainment industry.

Butterfly McQueen, who played Prissy in "Gone With the Wind," was a life-long atheist. She was a caring, generous individual who fought against racism and oppression. During a speech before the Freedom From Religion Foundation (of which she was a Life Member), she commented, "As my ancestors are free from slavery, I am free from the slavery of religion." Butterfly invested time and energy into cleaning up slums. "They say the streets are going to be beautiful in heaven," she observed. "I'm trying to make the streets beautiful here."

Freethinkers care about *this* world. We teach our children the basic human values of honesty, responsibility, fairness, kindness, intelligence, reason, and respect. We do not threaten eternal punishment or promise other-worldly rewards in order to manipulate people to live a life of values: natural consequences are all the motivation we need. To the unbeliever, good is good for good's sake alone.

On television we often observe many religious roles, reflecting the rich diversity of our nation. But characters who are openly atheistic, though common in society, are scarce on the screen. Identifiable atheists and agnostics are as underrepresented on TV as we are in the prison system. It is as if the television industry reflects not only religious diversity but the general religious assumption that it's not nice to be critical of religion.

No one should try to dictate what kinds of programs the television industry should produce; but if anyone asks for our opinion, we freethinkers think it would be nice to see some shows that are critical of religion, directly skeptical alternatives to the ubiquitous shows about angels, prayer, Noah's Ark, biblical archaeology, faith, and so on. We have noticed that the few times atheists or agnostics are given a chance to present their views, the producers bend over backwards to provide balance, putting ministers or religious experts on the same show. Rarely does it work the other way around.

For example, I was once a guest on Seattle's "Town Meeting" TV talkshow to discuss atheism. For "balance" the producers included a local Baptist minister, a Catholic priest, and a rabbi, who gobbled up most of the time proselytizing, saying nothing that we haven't already heard for centuries.

Fine. But on programs that deal with religion, freethinkers or skeptics are rarely invited to give the "other side."

It would also be illuminating to see some news programs spotlighting public officials who abuse their constitutional oath by using their office or tax money to promote religion. Alabama Judge Moore, a darling of the Christian Coalition, is fighting a lawsuit over the fact that he has a Christian prayer uttered before court sessions, and displays the Ten Commandments on his wall. Governor Thompson of Wisconsin, a Catholic, autocratically removed our legally placed "State/Church: Keep Them Separate" banner from the capitol rotunda, claiming that it doesn't reflect the "values" of Wisconsin citizens. Such anecdotes are ubiquitous.

On the positive side, there are many wonderful, entertaining stories that can be told involving people who are openly free from religion. How about a made-for-TV movie about Vashti McCollum, the woman who won a landmark Supreme

Court victory removing religious instruction from the public schools in 1948? This is a warm, human interest story about a brave unbelieving family defending "family values." Vashti's children were harassed and her family was shunned by the community when she stood up for the American principle of state/church separation. (Vashti's story can be read in her book *One Woman's Fight.*)

How about a show depicting the story of seven-year-old Mark Welch, who brought home a flier from public school inviting "any boy" to join the Boy Scouts? His father Elliott took him to the evening meeting at the school gymnasium and when the boys broke into groups, Elliott went to the table to sign Mark up. Noticing the Declaration of Religious Principle, he told the woman that his family was not religious and could not sign such a thing. "Then you'll have to leave," she told him coldly. Elliott had to go pull his son away from his friends, taking him out into the night, trying to explain why their family was not good enough for the Boy Scouts. (The Boy Scouts of America have defended this action in court, as well as many other cases of prejudice against unbelievers.)

Numerous brave and colorful freethinking champions have put their lives and reputations on the line in order to keep state and church separate. The struggle of the Unitarian family of Ed Schempp, whose famous 1963 Supreme Court *Schempp* decision removed prayer and bible reading from the public schools, is entertaining, poignant, and informative—and would make for a great television movie.

Or how about the fascinating life of the "great agnostic" Robert Green Ingersoll, the most famous orator of the nineteenth century, a warm family man and friend to presidents who has been virtually erased from history because of the manner in which he was vilified by the clergy for his iconoclastic views on religion? Or Thomas Paine, the deistic founding father, confidant of Washington and Jefferson, who wrote *Common Sense*, inspiring our country to a Revolutionary War, and who was later ostracized after writing *The Age of Reason*, the first American book critical of the Bible? Their stories would also make for great television fare.

Freethinking TV viewers would love to see a movie about Luther Burbank, the gentle "infidel" scientist who singlehandedly added billions in horticultural wealth to the world, and who was literally hounded to death by angry believers around the continent after his unbelief was revealed nationally. Or a documentary about the freethinking views of many of the early feminist pioneers such as Elizabeth Cady Stanton, who was shunned even by feminists after she wrote *The Woman's Bible,* critical of patriarchal religion. Or a show depicting how the irreverent humorist Mark Twain decided not to have his sacrilegious book *Letters from the Earth* published until long after his death because of the fear of religious reprisal.

Freethinkers have never bullied the entertainment industry with consumer boycotts or demands to present our point of view. The entertainment industry's only responsibility is to entertain.

I do suggest that the entertainment industry ought not to feel pressured by minority religious groups that complain that their particular views are being ignored or trivialized. Television has no obligation to preach the philosophy of any group of people, religious or not. If fundamentalist Christians want to hear about a "loving Jesus," they can turn on a religious channel, or turn off the TV and go to church. If they think their image needs improving, then they should start acting in ways to improve their image.

Let's face it: to most Americans, religion is boring. It makes many feel uncomfortable or embarrassed. It is insulting to others. You can show people sitting in a place of worship, praying to Jesus, Mary, Yahweh, or Allah, putting money in the collection plate, singing hymns. Then what? Writers can't carry it as far as the zealots would insist without turning television into tedium. Or worse, into sacrilege. Many believers don't want the "secular media" speaking on their behalf anyway.

Of course, sometimes religious expressions make sense in a show, in the context of plot and a character's motivation; but we freethinkers notice that gratuitous references to "God" or "heaven" are far too often sprinkled unnecessarily into the dialogue. Such casual comments may seem quite natural to Christians, but they are jarring intrusions to unbelievers. The assumption that all viewers understand the human race to be subservient to a Master and Lord is quite unsettling to millions of us who are free to think for ourselves.

We live in a country that is proudly rebellious. We fought a Revolutionary War in order to expel the King, Master, and Lord from our shores. We are not slaves to a dictator nor sinners deserving of eternal punishment. We are a country of "We, the people," the first nation with a godless constitution that is not based on the authority of a Sovereign. We freethinkers would never try to dictate the content of television programs, but we think producers and writers ought to know how unbelievers feel when we repeatedly see and hear references to the supernatural taken for granted, out of context, and not germane to the story.

If you can use religious comments for "color," then you could do the same with comments critical of religion. This will offend some viewers, but then we could all be offended equally.

Many television shows are purposely light in style and content, and it is understandable that certain religious or non-religious individuals will be caricatured in such programs. No discerning viewer should take offense. TV is not real life, after all.

But serious television programs should try to be accurate. Of course, not all fundamentalist Christians are hateful and intolerant and they should not always be portrayed that way. Neither are all unbelievers "angry atheists." Most freethinkers in America are happy, moral, productive, and tolerant.

Writers who create characters exemplifying goodness and charity should not jump automatically to ministers, priests, rabbis, Sunday School teachers, or missionaries. How about a "compassionate atheist" as a main character in a show promoting family values? Much good has been done in this world by people free from religion. And much harm has been committed by the clergy.

Millions of Americans are chagrined by the pretense that "family values" are an exclusive province of Christians or Jews, suggesting that the rest of us lack a compass for ethical behavior. Morality existed on this planet long before the Ten Commandments. Reason and kindness are all we need. We don't need a Bible or Lord to know how to live.

Jesus never used the word "family." He said, "If any man come to me, and hate not his father, and mother, and wife, and children, and brethren, and sisters, yea, and his own life also, he cannot be my disciple." He never married or fathered children, and actually discouraged parenthood (Matthew 19:12). To his own mother, Jesus said, "Woman, what have I to do with thee?" When a disciple requested time off for his father's funeral, Jesus rebuked him: "Let the dead bury their dead." These are hardly "family values."

Nowhere in the Bible do you find the warm-fuzzy nuclear family that modern American Christians champion.

Jesus said, "Think not that I am come to send peace on earth: I came not to send peace but a sword." The shameful litany of Christian oppression and warfare has fulfilled this prophecy. History and current headlines show that much evil has been committed in the name of religion. Are we all supposed to pretend otherwise?

If the television industry wants to be fair, then it should not always portray religion in a favorable light. For example, why did none of the broadcast media in the United States choose to air the critically acclaimed movie "The Boys of St. Vincent," spotlighting the serious epidemic of pedophilia among members of the Catholic priesthood? Does the Church still control the media as it did in the 1950s?

There will always be an unresolvable tension between religion and entertainment. Religion, by nature, is exclusionary and divisive; the entertainment industry, by necessity, must be inclusive and pluralistic. Most religions proselytize; good entertainment avoids preaching. Most religions teach that everyone in the world should be made to accept their values; good entertainment recognizes that the viewer has a choice.

Whether we believe in a supernatural world or not, those of us who care about *this* world agree that our society needs more understanding, more beauty, and less violence. Religion is not the answer. The answer lies in the responsible promotion of human values. Although we understand that the entertainment industry proclaims no mission to improve the world, there is no reason why it should feel pressured to perpetuate erroneous ideas that have made things worse.

6

On Bringing the Religious and Television Communities Together

A. James Rudin

Americans probably devote more of their leisure hours to participating in religious activities and to watching prime time television than to any other endeavors. But for too long, representatives of religion and prime time TV, two significant molders of public opinion, have acted as if they were the proverbial ships in the night that pass one another without being aware of each other's existence.

And when religion and prime time TV do encounter one another, it is, to use Matthew Arnold's popular and poignant poetic phrase: "Swept with confused alarms of struggle and flight, Where ignorant armies clash by night." It is clearly time to end the contentious relationship that often exists between religion and prime time television.

But, of course, the generals from both "armies" have their own explanations for this dreary state of affairs. Prime time TV, indeed, the entire entertainment industry, feels itself beleaguered and scapegoated stemming from the increasing criticism by religious zealots and ambitious politicians. TV representatives repeatedly claim their programs simply reflect much of contemporary America, and they deeply resent the accusation that they are somehow "anti-family" or "anti-religion."

Some entertainment leaders speak movingly about their personal efforts to transmit positive spiritual values to their own young children. One producer of a highly popular show has told me privately: "I'm from the heartland—Ohio. Many of my colleagues working in prime time TV in Los Angeles were also raised in Middle America. We're getting a bum rap."

But TV people are apprehensive about putting explicit religious themes into their programs lest they offend some particular group or denomination. Executives frequently lament that they can't do anything serious about abortion on prime time TV. No matter how the story ends, they believe they are the losers. And these same executives further maintain that it is difficult to have the clergy as major characters or in major roles on prime time—lawyers, doctors, police, teachers, and politicians, yes; but clergy, no.

Entertainment people declare that prime time TV can not present a "bad" or flawed member of the clergy; there will be too many complaints. Because of this self-imposed restriction, clergy on the tube are frequently limited to hatching, matching, and dispatching people.

And priests, rabbis, and ministers constantly and quite correctly point out that authentic religious experiences and activities are consistently omitted from prime time TV. And this despite the fact that, during any given week, many more Americans participate in synagogue and church programs than attend all the sporting events held during the same seven-day period.

Religious leaders from all faith communities believe it is simply unacceptable for America's extraordinarily rich and diverse religious life to be excluded from the world's single greatest instrument of entertainment, education, and communication: prime time TV. But despite their anger and dissappointment, most American religious leaders hold out a collective hand of friendship and cooperation to TV people. But with this extended hand also comes a warning and a hope.

The warning is that because prime time TV is such a powerful shaper of values, especially among young people, it may soon attract harsher scrutiny and condemnation for not representing something called "traditional American/religious values." When that happens, there will be many calls to "control the beast" of prime time TV.

And although it is primarily the extremists in the religious community who employ boycotts of offending programs and their commercial sponsors, and who circulate ugly black lists, even mainstream religious leaders may end up calling for a form of government censorship regarding TV program content.

The hope is that the TV industry will not abuse the enormous power that enables it to reach millons of people week after week. One way to avoid that is to engage in a specific ongoing program of consultation between the prime time TV and religious communities. Let me be clear: consultation and cooperation does not mean a religious veto or theological censorship over programming, but it does mean mutual respect and understanding.

Prime time TV needs many more expressions of authentic religious activities and values on its shows, and TV needs to "get it right" when it does portray American spiritual life. Clearly, the TV industry does have such consultative arrangements with the legal, medical, and law enforcement communities—three important sources for popular programming. The same kind of outreach needs to be developed with the religious community.

Because the communities affiliated with religion and prime time TV are both mature (each one has always had severe critics!), they can both be honest with one another. "Edgy" TV shows that honestly portray the reality of America's religious life, warts and all, are urgently needed and will even be welcomed by the religious community. And religion's empathetic critique of prime time TV is also urgently needed.

Both communities are strong enough to take each other's best punches, as well as warm hugs. But what neither religion nor prime time TV can endure are icy indifference and mutual hostility. The stakes are too high to let our "ignorant armies" continue to "clash by night."

Let a dynamic and fruitful encounter begin at last between our two communities of communication!

7

The Buddhist Perspective on Television Programming

Havanpola Ratanasara

In Buddhism, all persons, all individuals, have immediate and ultimate responsibility for the actions they take or do not take, the words they speak or do not speak, and the thoughts they think—their decisions. Therefore, mindfulness in thought, word, and deed is of utmost importance. Buddhists cannot apply to a "supreme being" for forgiveness or to assuage their consciences in the present or years later when they are facing death or enduring hard times. On a moment-by-moment basis, they strive to be mindful of what is wholesome or unwholesome in their lives. This affects their personal choices and the choices they make which affect others. If devout Buddhists are to watch a television program they would mindfully choose a program that would be educational, informative, or entertaining without being gross or offensive. Likewise in choosing what programs will be broadcast to the public, the mindful Buddhist would choose those programs which educate, inform, and entertain in a positive, wholesome way. They cannot shift the responsiblity to the public and say: "This is what they want to watch, what they will pay for." Broadcasting unwholesome programming, whether or not it is the choice of a segment of the viewing public, is still an unwholesome act on the part of those individuals who make the decision to broadcast the programs. And even if these programs are the choice of a segment of society, it is not only that segment of society that has access to the programs. Children at home without the benefit of their parents will also see this programming, draw the wrong conclusions, and be affected negatively. The negative effect on these young people who view some disturbing programming must be partially borne by those who made the decision to air the programs. For the Buddhist, the "effect" to be borne relates to the all-important karma, the accumulation of which for the wholesome or unwholesome will determine the condition of one's present life or future lives.

To the Buddhist it is clear that the network executives and program decision makers and the sponsors of unwholesome programming who say, "Don't blame us; it is what people want to see," are seeking self-exoneration and to shift the blame; but it cannot be shifted. The individual decision maker at each level is personally responsible and will suffer or enjoy the negative or positive karmic effect of his or her decision.

Parents and, to the extent that they are old enough to make a deliberate decision, children must also assume responsibility for negative results derived from watching negative programming. Determining what children watch and under what conditions is a major problem. Nor is it altogether clear what effect TV actually has on children. Many cartoons are filled with violence. Is it OK for loving, concerned parents to let their children watch hours of Saturday morning cartoons by themselves? It is said that parents should watch TV with their children, but, if they had to spend Saturday morning with the children, probably they could find something better to do with them than just sit and watch TV. Besides, to sit and draw lessons and put into perspective what is being seen takes a great deal of effort and may spoil the "entertainment" value of what is being watched, disrupt the concentration, and generally be a bother to both child and parent.

While instances of this parent-guided TV watching might be good for some occasions for short periods of time, it is not a practical solution to the overall problem. Obviously, it makes good common sense to go back to the other end of the process, to the decisions made by a few individuals, and solve the problem there rather than figure out how best to "control" the situation among millions of viewers, most of whom, on Saturday mornings, are children.

This is not an issue of censorship. It is an issue of individual ethics, of what has a good effect and what has an unwholesome effect on society. It is an issue of individuals making ethical or unethical decisions that may have wholesome or unwholesome effects on certain segments of society or society in general. It is a matter of individual decision makers dealing with the fact that "this is gratuitous violence for its own sake and I will not be a party to its being shown to millions of children," or "this is a distorted depiction of basic truths which fails to show the consequences of unethical behavior, and I will not make the decision to allow this to be produced (or aired) to the ultimate detriment of society." This is not censorship, it is the exercise of individual choice. Let those who wish to create such prurient, distorted programming go elsewhere to try to find a producer; let the negative effects of such programming fall on those less ethical and less caring. This is not censorship; it is saying: "I will have no part of producing this, look elsewhere!" And we can hope that, having looked elsewhere, the peddlers of trash, of unwholesome programming, will find no support.

There is no ethical mandate for a society to produce weapons for individuals to commit acts of murder, although there are those in society who choose to make their living producing these weapons. (In Buddhism, arms manufacturing and sales is considered an unwholesome occupation.) Likewise there is no ethical mandate for a society to produce depictions of gratuitous violence or inappropriate sexual acts for television just because there are some in society who want to see them.

The decision not to produce these depictions need not be forced by a government ban or widespread censorship; rather the decision should be made by individuals—not to write this material, not to produce it, not to air it, not to watch it. When individuals make decisions related to their own particular consciences and to their own personal job performance, this is individual, morally responsible ethics—not censorship.

This is also not about limiting free speech. Americans, as much as, if not more than, the citizens of any other country in the world, have the right to free speech. Buddhists, the ultimate individualists, enthusiastically endorse this. We should have the right to say what we want; but as socially ethical creatures we should not choose to exercise this right if what we say would be detrimental to the social good. Individuals may have the right to say things that will bring harm to others. But ethical individuals, truly mindful of their obligation to others, with respect for all life, with lovingkindness directed toward all, would never *choose* to say such things. In Buddhism individuals are tainted or purified, "saved" or "lost," made honorable or dishonorable, by their own acts, words, and thoughts—and for these, they alone are responsible. Thus for a Buddhist the question is never whether I have the right to act, say, or think something; the question for him or her becomes: "Is it ethical?" Freedom of speech (or action) is not the issue. Just so, in relation to television programming the question is not abridgment of freedom of speech but whether or not these individuals who are making the decisions about writing, producing, sponsoring, airing, and watching the programs, are individually acting in an ethically responsible manner. Are they considering the welfare of the children of the nation who may be misled, emotionally damaged, or encouraged to commit some evil act by the decision they are making to write, produce, sponsor, or air certain programming? And it is not just a public issue for these decision makers; it is a decision, the Buddhist believes, which determines the quality of his or her own present life and future lives as well. In fact, it can have incalculable consequences for many lives to come. For the sake of others as well as for themselves, such decisions cannot be taken lightly by mindful Buddhists.

Let us take this a step further to dramatize the issue in a Buddhist sense. Say that you are one of the members of a programming board responsible for airing a program which presents taking drugs as a glamorous, exciting, and generally acceptable thing to do, without showing the dire consequences of such a life style. This show then entices a youth to take up that life. Shortly thereafter that youth kills to satisfy his habit and is himself killed for not paying his drug debts. The consequences of these unwholesome, murderous acts would then become part of the karma for that individual committee member just as they would be a part of the karma of the actual drug addict and murderer. One cannot escape the karmic repercussions of any individual decision. If all decisions were mindfully made from this Buddhist perspective, we would have no worries about unwholesome programming.

In summary, from the Buddhist perspective, the problem of unwholesome television programming is a personal, individual issue; it is not a matter of censorship or of freedom of speech. It involves the decisions of individuals who write the programs, of individuals in corporate boardrooms of major networks who produce and air the programs, of individuals in commercial and business enterprises who sponsor the programming, and of individual station managers who decide whether or not to air the programs. It is with these individuals that the major responsibility lies; they are the ones whom the public can hold accountable. These are the individuals who are developing their own wholesome or unwholesome karma that affects their present and future lives. These are the individuals who are determining what type of programs are made available to the public. Although the decisions of the individual viewers have definite impact, they affect only the lives of themselves and their family members.

These individuals who have this heavy responsiblity, who have this great power to make these important decisions, should be made to understand their own personal ethical dilemma, the effect these decisions, even though made as a part of a board or committee, have on their own karma. Their names should be made known so that they cannot hide behind the corporate structure, so that they can be held individually and publicly accountable for their programming decisions, so that their individual consciences can be raised as they answer the tough questioning of the wronged public. Even if these individuals do not want to take the personal responsibilty for their decisions, the public will know and can take appropriate action such as writing letters or boycotting products. The burden need not be put on the parent or the child sitting in his or her own living room if the individual in the boardroom makes the wholesome decision. But even when the choice must be made in the living room as opposed to the boardroom, it is still an individual responsiblity and each one must be mindful of the implications for wholesome or unwholesome karma that his or her decision carries. If at each level the decision maker would adopt an attitude of loving kindness toward all others and acknowledge his or her ethical responsibility and the karmic consequences of his or her decisions, there would be no question of unwholesome programming.

III
Articles by
Academics

8

What You See Is What You Get:
Religion on Prime Time Fiction Television

Margaret R. Miles

The 1995 Conference on Religion and Prime Time Television focused on two primary complaints about television representation of religion. The first complaint was that the frequency with which prime time fiction television represents religion does not reflect Americans' present engagement with religion. The second complaint was that religion (especially Christianity) was represented too often as a negative or dangerous aspect of American culture, at best a partisan politics that constantly threatens to subvert loyalty to impartial public discourse. Prime time television was charged with depicting religion as inevitably partisan, self-promoting, and subversive of the common good of an increasingly pluralistic nation.[1] I will explore these complaints, endeavoring to identify the contribution of each as well as their ultimate inadequacy as cultural criticism. After discussing my approach to media analysis and exploring why these complaints do not, in my view, attend to the crucial issues surrounding media representations of religion, I will raise a different complaint. I will then make several suggestions for enhancing prime time programming's contribution to the public representation of religion in America.

At the risk of appearing to be the academic that I in fact am, I would like to begin by suggesting that a thorough analysis of media communications on the subject of religion requires the selective use of critical theories. Marxist, psychoanalytic, feminist, cultural studies, ideology critique, contextualist, representation theory: any of these could be useful for analysis of particular media communications. Although critical theory seems initially to be far removed from the practical concerns of television programming, its function is "to help individuals see and interpret phenomena and events."[2] Moreover, everybody has theories; expectations and assumptions direct what we notice and what we fail to see. But most of us, most of the time, do not acknowledge and examine our theories.

We are suspicious of theoretical approaches because we have seen them enslave and blind their adherents, rendering invisible anything not directly focused by the theory. Indeed, the capacity of theories to dominate vision is precisely the reason why theories must be used critically and interchangeably. Each theory illuminates a different segment of social reality, but must be jettisoned when it has reached its limits. Theories can best be thought of as a toolkit, as Michel Foucault suggested of his own theories.

Theory specifies what a reviewer assumes when he or she evaluates a cultural product so that the adequacy of those assumptions can be evaluated as well as the reviewer's conclusions. Only by the use of articulated and examined critical theories can we escape a positivist approach to the television "text." Positivist approaches rely on citing segments or episodes in a cultural product as evidence that topics such as religion have been represented, ignoring the complex medium, the cultural moment, and the economic arrangements through which the meaning of those represented incidents is mediated. Positivist analysis, in addition, denies that analysis is conducted in order to intervene, to change the objects of analysis.[3] In short, a more sophisticated analysis is needed than one which contends, from an undefined and falsely universal perspective, that a movie or television show produces "positive" or "negative" images of certain people or institutions.

Marxist analysis is needed for scrutinizing the economic arrangements surrounding particular depictions. Do advertising agencies have the final word in the content of prime time fiction television? Or do studio executives exercise power to determine what Americans should and should not see? Feminist or gender analysis is needed to expose the assumptions about gender roles and expectations operating in narrative programming. A theory of the way media representations function in American culture will direct us to analyze, not only a producer's intentions, but also the effects of media representations. An adequate theory of representation would, for example, overcome the naivete of the media worker who claimed, in one of the Conference panels, that merely showing a scene in a gay bar for thirty seconds did not imply approval of homosexuality but simply acknowledged its existence.[4] Finally, a contextualized cultural theory is required which places a television program or film in the cultural moment in which it was produced in order to detect its "resonant images," that is, images that resonate to a timely cultural experience, making them vibrant beyond their placement within the narrative.[5] In this essay I will endeavor to illustrate the usefulness only of the last of these critical theories.

The cultural studies approach I enlist as a critical lens understands media neither as a vehicle for deception and domination, nor as guileless entertainment, but as an arena of contested, negotiated, resisted, and appropriated meaning, a "contested terrain reproducing on the cultural level the fundamental conflicts within society."[6] Discussion of media's representation of religion, then, like discussion of any other topic, must be contextualized within the social and cultural "moment" in which it occurs.

RELIGION ON PRIME TIME AS REFLECTION OF AMERICAN SOCIETY

The first complaint about prime time fiction television's representation of religion assumes that media programming should reflect social conditions and interests more or less quantitatively. In the case of religion, the diverse forms of religion existing in American society should be represented in frequencies proportionate to the numbers of people they attract. While the simplistic version of this assumption is both impractical and mechanistic, there is, in my view, a kernel of insight within it that should not be lost. What the reflection theory brings to focus is that media entertainment, if it is to contribute to—as contrasted to escape from—discussion of the common social interests and anxieties of a broad range of Americans, must provide dramatizations that identify those interests and make proposals about them. The media fiction Americans watch is useful to the extent that it localizes and examines the perennial question of human life: How should we live?[7]

If some version of reflection theory were to become a criterion for prime time fiction programming's representation of religion, what could Americans expect to see? Critics of prime time programming often point to the increasing visibility of evangelical Protestants and Roman Catholics in America, urging more representation of evangelical Christians. But the picture of American religiousness they sketch is partial and therefore distorted. Demographic studies of religion in America show that Americans are becoming more religious, but in different configurations than formerly. According to statistics compiled from various sources, the largest religious populations other than Christianity in the United States are the following: [8]

Judaism	6 million
Islam	between 1 and 7 million
Buddhism	between 1 and 3 million
Hare Krishna	500,000
Hinduism	500,000
Christian Science	400,000
Neo-paganism	40,000

According to an extensive study of religious affiliation in the United States, only 9% of Americans profess no religion at all.[9] The figures I have cited are educated estimates; no one has yet counted these populations in a systematic way. However, approximate as these figures are, they reveal two important characteristics of contemporary American religiousness. First, that it is changing rapidly, and second, that it is changing in the direction of becoming more diverse. Religious pluralism is one important factor in any attempt to assess the reflective adequacy of representations of religion in America. This means that representations of minority religions occur in a volatile and, for many, anxiety-provoking religious social context, a context in which media representations can both inform and influence attitudes toward religious groups.

Within Christianity—still, in terms of numbers, clearly the predominant religion in the United States—there is also increasing diversity and change. The *Year-book of American and Canadian Churches*, which documents trends within Christianity, modestly designates itself a "snapshot of religious activity," since religious organizations are "in constant flux."[10] Mainstream Protestant denominations are declining: the Episcopal Church, the Evangelical Lutheran Church in America, the Presbyterian Church USA, the United Church of Christ, and the United Methodist Church.[11] On the other hand, considerable increases are occurring in the Roman Catholic Church, the Southern Baptist Convention, the Church of Jesus Christ of Latter-day Saints, and the Assemblies of God. The Pentecostal Church is presently the fifth largest denomination in the United States. Moreover, many members participate simultaneously in more than one church organization.

Christianity in the United States is also becoming less white. Two largely African American denominations are in the top seven in terms of membership size: the National Baptist Convention and the Church of God in Christ. Of the fourteen largest denominations, six have largely African American membership. Moreover, African Americans are apparently more religious than white Americans. By adding membership figures of predominantly African American denominations and estimates of African American participation in denominations with predominantly white membership, together with the one million plus African American Muslims, almost a hundred percent of the total African American population in the United States is accounted for.[12]

If a reflection theory of representation were adopted, it would need to present something resembling this religious picture. Although media workers object that it is impossible to please everyone with media representations of religion, programming that endeavored both to support those engaged in diverse religious groups by acknowledging their existence, and to inform Americans about the range of religious options presently available in the United States would seemingly rectify the purported problem of religion being underrepresented on prime time fiction television. But is this what those who complain of underrepresentation want? And would such carefully proportioned depictions of religion across network television be an adequate representation of religion in America?[13]

Before I address these questions another consideration deserves attention in relation to the complaint that prime time television does not reflect the numbers of Americans loyal to religion. The charge that religious commitment and motivation is excluded from prime time fiction broadcasting is becoming increasingly difficult to support. An analysis of almost two thousand hours of prime time programming conducted by the Media Research Center of Alexandria, Virginia, showed that in 1993 there were 116 portrayals of religion.[14] In 1994, the same group identified 253 portrayals of religion, more than twice the frequency of 1993 programming.[15] However, even cursory analysis of the Media Research Center's evaluations of prime time programming reveals the conservative religious perspective from which judgments were made.

Apparently, television programming has been affected by the conservative swing in the nation's mood. But when evangelical Christians say that they want to see favorable prime time fictional treatments of religion, it is "positive," or at least "neutral," treatments of conservative Christianity they want to see. They are not eager to entertain depictions of liberal Christianity; nor are they asking for increased fictional representations of the other religious groups presently attracting adherents in the United States. Conservative Christians seem also to assume that a broader discussion and negotiation of values—those "goods" of common life that people would like to be able to assume—can occur only under the rubric of religion, an assumption I will shortly question.

What do conservative Christians like to see in the entertainment media? The Christian Film and Television Commission's 1994 awards for the best films in the categories of "family picture" and "mature audiences" give an indication of the values that directed their choices. The best family picture was Walt Disney's "Homeward Bound: The Incredible Journey," "a movie starring two dogs and a cat." The best film for mature audiences was "The Remains of the Day." "The Age of Innocence" and "Much Ado About Nothing" were runners-up. The Commission denounced "Mrs. Doubtfire"; it was unacceptable because it "flaunts the admonition in Deuteronomy 22:5 that men not wear women's clothes."[16]

If the Christian Film and Television Commission accurately represents the Christian right, its approval and disapproval reveal a lack of recognition of the role of media in North American public life. The Commission awarded films that avoid offense—"nice" movies—rather than films that represent and explore the pressing problems of society. In other words, the Commission subscribes to the film industry's self-stylization as "entertainment," ignoring popular films' ability to represent conflicts of values for consideration, discussion, and negotiation.

The second complaint about prime time fiction television's representation of religion is that fiction media too often represent religion as dangerous and threatening to American public life and the common good. This contention, I believe, fails to acknowledge that such representations occur in a cultural moment in which religious extremists, fanatics, and zealots are both prominent in news media and frightening. That religious "lunatic fringes" exist and are dangerous to the common good has been documented too recently in living memory to be ignored. A society that has not forgotten Jonestown, and for whom images of the Branch Davidians' burning compound are still vivid, needs to explore, through media representation, the damage that can occur when powerful and totalitarian religious leaders are uncritically obeyed. Seen in relation to the cultural moment, representations of religion as dangerous are not difficult to understand. At such a moment, however, media might also contribute by providing images of forms of religion that remind secular America that religion is not monolithic, images that challenge religious people to cultivate their thoughtful exercise of moral responsibility in private and public spheres. This brings me to my complaint about depictions of religion and religious people on prime time fiction television.

RELIGION AS MONOLITHIC ON PRIME TIME TELEVISION

The two complaints against prime time television's representation of religion that I have discussed do not, in my view, go to the heart of the contradiction between Americans' various religious commitments and our commitment to secular public discourse. My complaint is rather that in endeavoring to pacify the Christian right by increasing depictions of conservative Christianity, entertainment media does not help Americans to recognize the complexity of religious commitment. Nor does it help them to discriminate between different religious perspectives in relation to issues concerning the common good. In fact, the label "Christian" has become synonymous with the Christian right.

It is exceedingly difficult for Christians who believe in the literal meaning of the King James Version of the Bible to talk with Christians who do not accept prooftexts, and who consider Biblical texts to be always in need of careful and contextual interpretation. But in relinquishing "Christian" as a description of their concerns and loyalties, liberal Christians permit the category to become monolithic in public usage. Prime time television largely reflects—and supports—the constriction of "Christian" to conservative, countercultural Christianity.

Liberal Christians and minority religious groups who find the religious right dangerously united on some crucial issues must define thoughtful positions on the same issues and thus demonstrate the variety of approaches consonant with Christian belief and practice. In my view, it is important to press on the public agenda religion that holds at its core commitment to social and institutional change on behalf of those who are impoverished, marginalized, and oppressed. This gospel stands in dramatic contrast to a gospel of the "straight and narrow way" that insists on adherence to particular social and sexual arrangements and behaviors. To date, conservative Christians have had a higher profile in pressing so-called "family values" in the name of their religious commitment than have liberal Christians. It would, of course, be helpful to see the complexity of diverse religious commitments examined in prime time programming.

Religions other than Christianity are similarly diverse. Islam, which is rapidly becoming the second most populous religion in America, is perhaps the most extreme example of monolithic representation of religion in American media.[17] While numerous examples of the abuse of religious ideas can be cited from every world religion, Muslims have become the suspects of choice in the 1990s. Muslims are currently represented in the communication media primarily as intolerant and monomaniachal terrorists. Many examples could be given; I will confine myself to one. In the first CBS news reports of the Oklahoma City federal building bombing, Middle Easterners were identified as the likely perpetrators. Their religion was immediately implicated in these suspicions: film clips were shown of Moslems praying at a convention in Oklahoma City the summer before, implying without stating that the bombing was related to Muslims' religious commitments. Such racial and religious media scapegoating has real effects: in the aftermath of the bombing, Middle Eastern Americans in many different cities suffered harassment and persecution.

I will conclude by suggesting briefly some directions prime time fiction television might explore in order to address more effectively the role of religion in America.

1. In the context of change and increasing diversity in Americans' religious commitments, accurate and sympathetic information about religions in America is of great importance. Lacking studies of the ratio of representations of Christianity to those of other religions, my informal observation suggests that conservative Christianity receives most of the prime time cultural space devoted to religion. Presumably this occurs both because the Christian right has been the most active of any religious group in protesting television's representation of religion, and because of the numerical dominance of conservative Christianity. However, the very fact that Christianity is numerically dominant indicates that many Americans may have little information about the beliefs, practices, lifestyles, rituals, and values of those of other religions. Without such information, prejudice and stereotype all too easily fill the gap. Moreover, if media representations are to be accurate and nuanced, practitioners of Buddhism, Islam, and Judaism, as well as Native American and other less populous religions, will be needed as consultants.

2. Prime time fiction television could increase and diversify representations of people who are endeavoring to live lives informed by religious and/or value commitments. Such programs would not focus on religious aspects of characters' lives but would depict these characters as ordinary Americans for whom religious commitment plays a role in decisions and relationships. One of the media's most prominent capacities is that of "naturalizing" certain behaviors by depicting them casually as part of daily life. The media that regularly naturalizes violence and other irresponsible and destructive behavior might contribute to American society by naturalizing the resources of religious faith.

3. Although the Christian right seems to assume that discussion and negotiation of values must occur in the context of depictions of religion, it is important, in a society that considers itself privately religious but commitedly secular in the public sphere, to recognize that value conflicts do not always occur in the context of religion. Traditionally, in societies of the like-minded, religion has defined, imposed, or attracted people to common values; but American society can no longer assume religious like-mindedness. For many Americans, a secular public sphere guarantees an arena of public discussion free from parochial interests.[18] It is important, then, frequently to depict confrontations of values as occurring outside the sponsoring arena of religion, as prime time fiction programming already regularly does.

4. Finally, there can be no substitute for training Americans in the skills of critical viewing. Although academic statements of critical theories can be relatively inaccessible, critical viewing is not necessarily so esoteric. A four-year-old can grasp the concept that the narrative of a television program or a movie has been made up by someone, and could be imagined differently. An older child can easily detect the race, class, or gender perspective from which a particular pro-

gram is presented and can learn to question the relationship of advertising segments to the program. Because, as Roland Barthes once said, audiences "get" the cultural message when they get the pleasure, analysis of one's viewing pleasure can be the starting place for such analysis.

Children are usually willing to think both more profoundly and more playfully about entertainment than are adults, who often claim that a favorite program is "spoiled" by analysis. Adults are so oriented to entertainment as a feature of their lives that it is, by definition, not to be thought about that they are typically more resistant to learning the considerable pleasures of critical analysis than are children. Moreover, since the media is presently such a large part of Americans' leisure activity, media literacy should be taught in public schools. For people who have developed critical attention to media, prime time fiction television programming can become the occasion for an exercise in considering proposals addressed to the essentially religious question, "How should we live?"

For facilitating consideration of this question, television dramas that present diverse characters in complex situations, working with various religious and values commitments, are a richer resource than are shows that feature conventional characters in simplified dilemmas. That complex dramas are more difficult to produce, more likely to draw attacks from the Christian right, and probably also find it more difficult to attract advertisers should also be acknowledged. Media workers' focus on offending as few people as possible is understandable, but it is also a fundamentally weak position from which to create drama. Prime time fiction television would serve religion well if, instead of fearing to offend, it represented religion in America as diverse, complex, and, like other aspects of life in the United States at the end of the twentieth century, always in need of critical examination.

NOTES

1. Jeffrey L. Sheler, "Spiritual America," *U.S. News and World Report*, April 4, 1994, p. 49.

2. Douglas Kellner, *Media Culture: Cultural Studies, Identity, and Politics between the Modern and the Postmodern* (New York: Routledge, 1995), p. 24.

3. Ben Agger, *Cultural Studies as Critical Theory* (Washington, D.C.: Falmer Press, 1992), p. 135.

4. Media representations of sexual, religious, and racial minorities begin to weave minority people into the mainstream of American society. People unused to seeing representatives of their group in media's reality-creating discourse are validated by such representations. In my view, this is one of the reasons it is important to represent a more inclusive range of our pluralistic society in prime time fiction television. On the other hand, those who object to the representation of sexual orientation minorities do so because they understand the validating power of the media.

5. The term "resonant images" is Kellner's (*Media Culture*, p. 107). One example of a resonant image might be "Thelma and Louise." In its conclusion, the film condemned those female outlaw buddies by outnumbering and outmaneuvering them with police cars (representative of patriarchal culture) that literally drove them into the Grand Canyon. But in the

body of the film, the image of Louise shooting the oil truck whose driver had made obscene gestures and used obscene language was a resonant image for millions of American women who suffer a high and constant level of daily public sexual harassment. Women who loved the movie loved it not for its ending but for such images of female outlaw freedom.

6. Kellner, *Media Culture*, p. 101-102.

7. Martha Nussbaum has described the origin of this question in ancient Greek public "entertainment" in *Love's Knowledge* (New York: Oxford University Press, 1990), p. 4 and *passim*.

8. See J. Gordon Melton, ed., *Encyclopedia of American Religion*, 4th edition (Washington, D.C.: Gale Research, Inc., 1993); also his *Religious Bodies in the United States: A Directory* (New York: Garland, 1992) and *Encyclopedic Handbook of Cults in America* (New York: Garland, 1992); and Charles H. Lippy and Peter W. Williams, eds., *Encyclopedia of the American Religious Experience: Studies of Traditions and Movements* (New York: Charles Scribner's Sons, 1988). The "Pluralism Project" at Harvard University, under the direction of Professor Diana Eck, will soon publish more accurate figures than are presently available, based on a systematic count of religious populations other than Christianity and Judaism in the United States.

9. Sheler, "Spiritual America," p. 50.

10. Kenneth B. Bedell, *Yearbook of American and Canadian Churches* (Nashville, TN: Abingdon Press, 1994), "Introduction."

11. Bedell, *Yearbook*, p. 12.

12. Bedell, *Yearbook*, "Introduction."

13. I assume that the criterion of balance between or among depictions of various religions within a single program is impossible to achieve. Such a criterion would also effectively prevent representation of *any* religion in any depth or complexity.

14. According to the Media Research Center of Alexandria, Virginia, 42.2% of the representations of religion were negative, while 30.2% were neutral portrayals, and 27.6% were positive representations. However, depictions rated (by whom?) as "negative," "neutral," or "positive" do not specify the criteria by which these evaluations are reached, thereby masking the assumed universal perspective engaged in such judgments. It is likely that a representation of Christianity that a fundamentalist Christian might find "positive" might appear to be highly "negative" to a liberal Christian. Thomas Johnson and Sandra Crawford, "Faith in a Box: Entertainment Television on Religion, 1994" (Alexandria, VA: 1995), p. 1.

15. Moreover, in the estimation of this conservative organization, in 1994, "friendly" depictions of religion outnumbered negative ones by almost 2 to 1, the reverse of 1993. "Faith in a Box, 1994," p. 1.

16. "The Envelope, Please," *The New York Times*, March 12, 1994. Religious News Service reports that 72% of the top 25 box office movies were "acceptable" to the Christian Film and Television Commission headed by Ted Baehr.

17. See Kellner's Chapter 6, "Reading the Gulf War: Production/Text/Reception," in *Media Culture*.

18. See Michael Suman, "Do We Really Need More Religion on Fiction Television?" (Chapter 11 in this volume) for an argument that "television is not about mirroring reality," and that religion is best understood and practiced in the private sphere. Suman fears that public exposure of religion could eventuate in a resurgence of the intolerance and bigotry that the Constitution seeks to forestall by separating religious and state powers. His argument assumes, however, that the loudest voices in support of public depictions of religion, the Christian right, would achieve hegemony over public broadcasting if more religion were to be televised. If the goal were to present a variety of living and accessible religious

options rather than to permit conservative Christianity to dominate, Suman's argument founders.

9

Reflections on Culture Wars: Churches, Communication Content, and Consequences

Judith M. Buddenbaum

> I inform the proud Moslem people of the world that the author of *The Satanic Verses*, which is against Islam, the Prophet and the Koran, and all those involved in its publication who were aware of its contents, are sentenced to death. I ask all Moslems to execute them quickly wherever they are found so that no others dare to do such a thing. Whoever is killed doing this will be regarded as a martyr and will go directly to heaven. (Ayatollah Ruhollah Khomeini, from a statement broadcast on Tehran Radio, February 14, 1989)

When the Ayatollah Ruhollah Khomeini issued that edict sentencing the novelist Salman Rushdie to death, people around the world, including many Moslems, were horrified. In America, bookstores quickly pulled copies of *Satanic Verses* from their shelves out of fear for the safety of their employees and customers, but then quickly restocked them in reaction to public demand.

"We are much too civilized to tolerate any such blatant attack on a mere novelist for writing mere words. Nothing like that could happen here," Americans proudly told each other. But could it?

Americans have a love-hate relationship with their mass media, and particularly with television. On the one hand, the average home has at least two television sets; in the majority of them a set is turned on six or more hours a day. More people say watching television is their favorite way to spend an evening than name any other single pastime. But even as they applaud television for providing information, they worry endlessly about its effects on themselves, their children, and on society. [1]

Such worries inform many people's private decisions about which programs to watch and which to avoid. Frequently those worries are expressed more publicly as constructive criticism of media fare. But sometimes reactions go beyond the kind of reasoned discourse the First Amendment guarantee of freedom of belief and expression was meant to encourage. While few would publicly call for killing the messenger,[2] many would, indeed, kill the messenger's message.[3]

In those reactions many have come to see evidence of a culture war—a struggle "to control . . . the 'instrumentality' of reality definition"—led by religious people who feel their deeply held values are under attack from a profit-driven information and entertainment industry that is a-religious at best, anti-religion at worst.[4] And there is some merit in that portrayal.

While few within the media industries would agree that their intent is to destroy traditional values, few would deny that artists and producers, protected by the First Amendment, frequently provide fare that ignores, denigrates, or at least raises questions about everything that many religious people hold dear. As research in both the cultivation[5] and agenda-setting[6] traditions show, in so doing the media have some ability to shape society.

Surveys conducted over the past fifty years show that Americans have generally become less prejudiced and more tolerant; however, that tolerance is still quite limited when it comes to criticism of religion and of cherished religious beliefs and values. Consistent with Hunter's "culture wars" analysis,[7] people who identify with a religion and consider it very important to them are significantly less tolerant than those who do not identify with any religion. However, most Jews are as tolerant as those with no religion; mainline Protestants and Catholics are generally more tolerant than conservative Protestants. At the same time, there are differences between Jews and Christians and among members of the various Christian traditions in what they will and will not tolerate.[8]

Therefore, Hunter's description of a culture war being waged between "religious" and "secular" camps may be oversimplified. As Wuthnow contends,[9] the "struggle to define America" may really stem from different views of the Bible and different styles of moral reasoning. Although religious people have no monopoly on media criticism, much criticism is, indeed, grounded in religious beliefs. And when it is, it can be particularly hard to refute or even placate, for the criticism is often presented as God's command, even though people who say they believe in the same God can be found both condemning and applauding the same media fare.

In an effort to understand what churches that ostensibly represent the same religion—Christianity, as the dominant religion in America—say about the mass media and to gauge their reactions to particular kinds of media fare, students in my fall 1994 freshman seminar on religion and the media sent questionnaires to the top leader in each of the 209 Christian churches in the United States listed in the 1993 *Yearbook of American and Canadian Churches*.[10] Information in this article is based on those leaders' answers to questions tapping opinions about television and about support for expressive rights.

The church leaders who received the questionnaire were asked to answer the questions on the basis of official church positions or, if the church had no such position, "the way you believe most religious leaders from your church would answer them." Usable replies came from 65 of the churches surveyed. The replies from those 65 churches cannot be considered a census of all Christian churches or even a representative sample although they include approximately equal numbers of responses from Pentecostal, other Fundamentalist, Evangelical, mainline Protestant, and Catholic churches, both eastern- and western-rite. Still, their replies provide useful insight into the relationship between religion and media criticism and the problems for the media and for society embedded within that criticism.

GRADING TELEVISION ENTERTAINMENT

Well over half of the mainline Protestant and Catholic leaders labeled mass media either "appropriate" or "very appropriate" as a source of entertainment for members of their churches; none labeled them "very inappropriate." However, leaders from mainline Protestant churches considered the mass media significantly more appropriate sources of entertainment than did more conservative Protestant or Catholic leaders (see Table 9.1).

When asked to rate individual media, church leaders were somewhat more likely to consider television appropriate (x = 1.8 on a 3-pt. scale) than popular music (x = 1.6), or movies (x = 1.4), but they tended to rate television as somewhat less appropriate for members to use for entertainment than either radio (x = 2.1) or books (x = 2.8). Half of the Evangelical respondents and one-third of those from Catholic churches labeled television the least appropriate entertainment medium, as did as many as one-fifth of those from other Christian traditions. In comparison, more than two-thirds of the Pentecostal, other Fundamentalist, and Evangelical respondents and one-third of those representing various Catholic churches labeled movies the least appropriate; more than three-fourths of the respondents from those groups labeled books the most appropriate form of entertainment. Most mainline respondents agreed that books are most appropriate, but none called movies the least appropriate entertainment medium.

When they were asked to assign traditional letter grades to mass media performance, fewer than one-fourth of the respondents from each tradition considered

Table 9.1
Appropriateness of Mass Media Use for Entertainment by Christian Tradition

Tradition	Very Inapp.	Inapp.	Neither	App.	Very App.
Pent. (n = 13)	7.7	15.4	46.2	23.1	7.7
Fund. (n = 19)	21.1	10.5	15.8	42.1	10.5
Evan. (n = 16)	—	6.3	25.0	50.0	18.8
Main. (n = 10)	—	—	30.0	10.0	60.0
Cath.* (n = 5)	—	—	20.0	—	80.0

Chi square, 31.53, df 16; Cramer's V = .354; p = .01.
* This category includes Orthodox and western-rite churches including the Roman Catholic church.

mass media entertainment satisfactory. Although 3 gave B's and there were 11 C's, the average grade was a D ($x = 2.07$ on a 5-pt. scale). There were 26 D's and 21 F's. Leaders from eastern- and western-rite Catholic churches were somewhat more lenient in their grading, giving the media a solid D+ ($x = 2.4$), and Evangelicals were somewhat more critical, giving them a D- ($x = 1.6$), but the differences among groups were not statistically significant with this small sample.

As abysmal as those grades were, they were better than the D- ($x = 1.4$ on a 5-pt. scale) grades these church leaders gave for the way entertainment media portray religion. Catholics and mainline Protestants judged the portrayal as a D- ($x = 1.7$); Pentecostals gave it an F ($x = 1.2$), but again the differences were not statistically significant. Only one church leader awarded a grade of B; there were 4 C's, but 15 D's and 42 F's.

EXPLAINING THE GRADES

Comments that church leaders wrote on their questionnaires suggest that dissatisfaction stems from a general feeling that entertainment media generally ignore and denigrate religion in all its myriad forms while at the same time they provide fare that seems to church leaders designed to undermine the very values and behaviors these leaders cherish.

The depth of such feelings can be seen from the fact that 50 of the 65 respondents took the time to answer questions asking them to explain the grades they gave the entertainment media. Both the complaints and the language used in voicing them were remarkably similar across religious traditions. Leaders generally decried the lack of serious attention to religion and to its importance and value for many people. As one respondent from an Evangelical church put it, "The appearance is that it is largely irrelevant in life; yet a large percentage of the population is religious." Others agreed:

When it's shown, it's a joke. (Pentecostal leader)

Religion is either satirized, made fun of or ignored: seldom ever taken seriously. (Fundamentalist leader)

Religion is shown as peripheral to mainstream life, or is a joke. (Evangelical leader)

Mostly they ignore religion—when they do portray religion, it is often incompetent, humorous, irrelevant or sloppy. (Mainline leader)

It is either too little or too negative. (Catholic leader)

In such comments, one can see a widespread desire for more attention to religion and more favorable portrayals of religious people and religious institutions. One mainline Protestant leader wrote, "Religious people and institutions [are] often caricaturized or stereotyped, but, worse, often are missing altogether." Similarly, a Fundamentalist leader commented that the media provide "predominantly (almost exclusively) negative representations" and "play on the lowest common denominator," while an Evangelical added that they are "too negative toward religion, or totally ignore the value of such."

A few attributed what one mainline leader called a "strong bias against all real religious efforts" to a general lack of understanding about religion on the part of media professionals. One Evangelical linked a "sometimes hostile" media to "shallow understanding." A Catholic leader wrote, "I am disturbed [that] these people who write on religion know so little about it," and a mainline Protestant added, "The little attention given religion is almost always focused on negative aspects . . . stereotypes. Few script writers take time to do research and get it right."

Some respondents, including people from both very small and very large churches in each tradition, said their religion has been portrayed in entertainment fare less often and less favorably than others; others said their religion is portrayed more often and more favorably. While there were no differences in perception by religious tradition, and those perceptions of how much and how well their church has been portrayed were unrelated to judgments about the media, comments suggest many leaders are more concerned about their own religion than about others.

Almost all complained about what they saw as an "anti-Christian bias" in entertainment programming, but here there were differences between liberal and more conservative complaints. Conservative Protestants believed the media focus on conservative Christianity, but comments such as "Our denomination is Evangelical in practice; we are the object of scorn," and "Our church is ultra conservative; the entertainment media currently is [sic] ultra liberal" suggest they see it as evidence of a deliberate "liberal slant." Mainline Protestants agree that the media "often rel[y] on the fringes of religious groups rather than mainstream or liberal groups," but they fear that "narrow portrayals" that "focus on the religious right" create the impression that "fundamentalism is the 'normal' American religious way."

Only one leader, from a mainline Protestant church, noted that Christians are generally portrayed more often and more favorably than non-Christians. Two said the media "try to be fair" to all religions and do "fairly well," but an Evangelical respondent saw more problems with the way the media depict Jesus than with the way they portray Mohammed or Buddha.

Pleas for religious "truth" instead of "fiction" were common. "They hide under the cloak of 'fiction,' " one mainline Protestant leader complained. A Pentecostal leader wrote, "Most religious stories, etc., [are] made for TV audiences and not the real truth." As that comment suggests, many church leaders, particularly those from conservative Protestant churches, would like the media to define religious truth the way they do. Complaints about "anti-biblical—thus anti-Christian" bias were common. "They either blaspheme or misinterpret the Bible," one Evangelical leader lamented.

Only a few comments such as the one from another Evangelical leader who wrote, "Most of what gets through is self-righteous instead of justification by faith in Christ Jesus," were clear about the "misinterpretations" they find offensive. For most, concern for upholding religious truth was less directly connected to specific church teachings than to the fear that story lines encourage ideas and behaviors that undermine morality.

Some respondents acknowledged that television entertainment isn't all bad. At least one respondent from each tradition mentioned "Christy" as a "bright spot." One mainline Protestant identified public television as a source of quality programming. Probably very few would go as far as the Fundamentalist who wrote, "Because a large percent of the programs featured on radio and television are of an evil nature, we do not tolerate them," but many might agree with one who said that "much entertainment is not appropriate for human consumption."

Almost all echoed, in one way or another, the opinion of another Fundamentalist leader who wrote that there is "very little good quality entertainment." One mainline leader noted "large scale disillusionment with the quality of much entertainment media" stemming primarily from the perception that there is too much sex and violence on television. Altogether 15 respondents mentioned sex; 16 mentioned violence. Several mentioned "foul language" or "profanity"; one Evangelical leader criticized "negative quality music and lyrics"; another singled out "moronic sitcoms," while another worried specifically about the effect of "sitcoms, music and talk shows [that] debunk and ridicule religious values and people."

In those replies, and many others, the concern for effect was obvious. One Evangelical leader went so far as to call entertainment programs "moral crap." But like bias, "moral crap" may be in the eyes of the beholder. Although almost half of all respondents asked for programs supporting religious values, again there were differences between the comments from Catholics and conservative Protestants, on the one hand, and more liberal Protestants on the other.

Both Catholic and conservative Protestant leaders mentioned violence, but for them the major problem was clearly sexually oriented programming which undermines "traditional" or "Biblical morality" and "family values." Much "programming seems to favor immorality," a Catholic leader wrote. "Too much violence, sex, and very little emphasis on integrity, moral values, or family values," a Fundamentalist added. Believing portrayals of "immoral lifestyles," "anti-Christian homosexuality" and "perversity," "adultery, promiscuity, etc." teach viewers that such behaviors are common and normal, they criticized programs for being "anti-Biblical" and for promoting "situation ethics."

Mainline Protestant leaders also noted an overabundance of entertainment fare featuring sex and violence, but their concern was not with sex and violence per se. Rather, they complained about "gratuitous violence," "sexual violence," and "irresponsible" and "exploitive sex," as well as programs that "glorify cruelty, exploitation, ugliness." One voiced a concern for "traditional values," but others were more concerned about "shallow programs" that fail to encourage "real freedom of thought" because they are "too uncritical of institutions [and] ignore larger moral and ethical perspectives." They wanted "images of Christians fighting for justice" and worried that programs encourage stereotyping and discrimination against disadvantaged groups. In sharp contrast to the conservative Protestants, one mainline leader specifically said there are not enough "positive images of gays, lesbians, and other minorities."

PROTECTING FREEDOM OF EXPRESSION

Although assessments of the grades the media deserve for the quality of the entertainment they provide and the way they portray religion in entertainment fare were similar across Christian traditions, the differences that emerged as they explained their grading support the idea of a culture war. How important that war may be to at least some churches and how far they may go in an effort to control the symbols that portray and, perhaps, define American culture can be seen in church leaders' responses to a series of questions asking whether various kinds of expression should always, sometimes, or never be protected by law (see Table 9.2).[11]

Across all Christian traditions, leaders said they wanted more and more favorable attention to religion in television programming, but many of their comments suggested that they were most concerned that their own religion be portrayed as true and valuable. Consistent with that interpretation, Catholic and conservative Protestant leaders were generally more inclined to grant at least some protection to expression that offends other people because of their religion than to speech that contradicts the teachings of their own religion. Most would give at least some protection to examinations of church finances; almost as many would give some protection to speech that offends other religions. But at least half of the conservative Protestant leaders and almost as many Catholics were unwilling to extend any protection to those whose differing beliefs might lead them to say things these leaders find sacrilegious, i.e., contrary to their own religious beliefs.

Most Catholics and conservative Protestants said graphic news photos depicting violence should have some legal protection, but they were generally less willing to extend that protection to portrayals of other kinds of behaviors. Catholic leaders were generally unwilling to protect portrayals of drug use, nudity, homosexuality, or the showing of X-rated movies which would, of course, receive that rating for sex and/or violence, but most were at least as inclined to protect material that might be considered presentations of alternative lifestyles as they were to protect expressions of alternative religious views. However, conservative Protestants were generally less willing to protect depictions of drug use and sexuality than they were to protect alternative religious viewpoints. Indeed, no Pentecostal leader would give any legal protection to music videos showing drug use or to X-rated movies. Only one would protect television shows portraying homosexuality. Among other Fundamentalists, only two or three would give any protection to portrayals of drug use, nudity, or homosexuality.

In contrast to those views, mainline Protestant leaders were significantly more likely than those from other Christian traditions to protect all kinds of speech. Unlike the Catholic and conservative Protestant leaders, they were more inclined

Table 9.2
Mean Scores on Support for Expressive Rights by Christian Tradition

	Pentecostal	Fundamentalist	Evangelical	Mainline	Catholic
Religion					
Sacrilege	1.50[a]	1.53[a]	1.73[a]	2.75	1.67[a]
Teaching evolution	1.50[a]	1.50[a]	1.80[a]	3.00	1.83[a]
Satanic lyrics	1.23[a]	1.26[a]	1.73	2.13	1.67
Offending other religions	1.85	1.74[a]	1.93	2.50	1.83
Expression					
Examinations of church finance	2.15[a]	2.33[b]	2.20[a]	2.89	1.67[a]
Lifestyles					
Music videos showing drug use	1.00[a]	1.21[a]	1.67[c]	2.00	1.67[c]
X-rated movies in theaters	1.00[a]	1.32[a]	1.60[a,c]	2.56	1.83[c]
Nudity in magazines	1.31[a]	1.63[a]	1.67[a]	2.78	1.67[a]
Homosexuality in TV shows	1.08[a]	1.37[a]	1.56[a,c]	2.67	1.67[a,c]
Graphic news photos of violence	1.69[a]	1.79[a]	2.00	2.50	2.00

Note: Mean scores are on a 3-pt scale: 1 = never protect; 2 = sometimes protect; 3 = always protect. Differences among groups (p = .05) are based on a one-way analysis of variance: [a] Groups differing from mainline Protestants; [b] Groups differing from Catholics; [c] Groups differing from Pentecostals.

to protect speech that is sacrilegious toward their own religion than that which might offend other people because of their religion. However, they also said that teaching of evolution, which is contrary to the beliefs of other Christians, should always be protected by law. Only on the matter of protecting satanic lyrics and music videos showing drug use were they somewhat ambivalent. At least half would always protect graphic photos of violence, nudity in magazines, homosexuality in television programs, and X-rated movies.

CONSEQUENCES AND CONCLUSIONS

Almost unanimously the church leaders who replied to our survey criticized the entertainment media for their overemphasis on sex and violence. In place of such fare, they wanted more programs suitable for viewing by the entire family. As part of that, they called for greater sensitivity to religion and religious values. Underlying that concern is the widespread belief that entertainment fare, and particularly television programming, is responsible both for a decrease in religiosity and for increased criminal and immoral behavior.

Such fears are real, although the threat may be overblown. Church adherence is more than three times higher than it was in colonial America. And while the stigma may be less today than it was in the days of Nathaniel Hawthorne's *Scarlet Letter*, single women in Puritan New England were more likely to be sexually active than to belong to a church.[12] Surveys indicate church attendance and the proportion of people saying their religion is very important have generally inched upward since the turn of the century.[13]

At the same time, some crime rates are up; others are down. But overall, they are no higher today than they were before World War II. Annual homicide rates compiled by the U.S. Department of Justice show that homicides have doubled since 1950, but the sharpest increase occurred before World War II when it rose from about 2.5 per 100,000 people in 1905 to almost 10 per 100,000 in 1933. During the war, the homicide rate was only about half of what it had been during Prohibition, but after the war the rate again climbed, reaching prewar levels in the mid-1970s. Since then, it has held rather constant, albeit with some annual fluctuation.

However, none of that means that church leaders' fears are without merit. Messages do have consequences. To argue otherwise would, in effect, be saying that communication is a meaningless activity. Although causal links are less clear, more than fifty years of media research provide evidence of correlations between media content and media effects that underscore the validity of clergy concerns.[14]

Therefore, those responsible for programming—as corporate owners, advertisers, producers, directors, writers, and entertainers—need to consider what they are doing. If their own sense of ethics and integrity does not motivate them to take into account the possible effects of the body of their work on individuals and on society, then they should at least be concerned for very pragmatic reasons. Failure to limit sex and violence and to provide in its place more family-friendly fare may lead to increasing pressure for government regulation that would, by its very nature, undermine cherished First Amendment freedoms.

But with or without government regulation, the potential exists for serious economic consequences. As organizations, churches have both the infrastructure and the committed memberships that make mobilization possible. Clergy-led calls for bans and boycotts are common; they can be quite successful. But even churches that would not seek to remove from the airwaves material they find offensive can be quite persuasive at convincing their members to look elsewhere for entertainment. Thus, they too can affect the bottom line because of the relationship between viewership and advertising dollars.

However, saying that the television industry should—indeed must—be sensitive to church complaints is the easy part. Television can easily cut back on programs featuring sex and violence, but the shows that replace them must still be about something. And therein lies the dilemma.

Everyone says they want more programs that in movie rating terms would earn a G. Although there is less evidence that their members would actually watch such programs,[15] a steady bill of such fare would undoubtedly satisfy many conservative Protestant clergy. It would not, however, avoid criticism from mainline Protestants whose complaints about sex and violence are frequently coupled with pleas for more thought-provoking programs and for less stereotyping and negative portrayals of minorities, including homosexuals. Acting on mainline Protestants' desires could produce programs deeply offensive to many of their fellow Christians, just as programming that consistently supports conservatives' religious beliefs and their concept of morality could offend mainline Protestants as well as those who are not Christian.

In their open-ended comments and in their stronger support for expressive rights, mainline Protestants are expressing opinions consistent with their religious convictions just as surely as are Catholics and the more conservative Protestants who frequently complain about "anti-Biblical" material that undermines "traditional values." Where conservative Protestants, and to some extent Catholics, tend to define "morality" in terms of personal behaviors and particularly individual sexual behaviors, mainline Protestants, as well as many Catholics, see sin primarily in actions that exploit or marginalize other people.

But more importantly, it is the mainline Protestant insistence on the primacy of individual conscience and reason that makes the culture war as much a clash of religions as a war between religion and the supposed secularism of the media industry. Where most mainline Protestants would agree with Milton[16] and Mill[17] that people are rational and that they can and will find truth through its clash with error, Catholics give more credence to the teaching authority of the church than to individual conscience and reason. Conservative Protestants are even less sanguine about human nature. For them, a literally true and inerrant Bible is the sole authority.[18]

Because of the importance they attach to a marketplace of ideas, mainline Protestants are, in many ways, mass media's natural allies. However, it is important to remember that "tolerance for" is not the same thing as "acceptance of."[19] The same churches that would tolerate nudity in magazines and X-rated movies in theaters might find them quite unacceptable on television which comes into their homes, even with V-chips that could be used to prevent their children from seeing such programs. In recent years, mainline churches have coupled criticism of television programming with barely veiled calls for greater government regulation, both to protect children and to increase availability of the kinds of programs they favor.[20]

Although the government regulation they sometimes advocate would inexorably affect the kinds of programs that could legally be shown on prime time television, to date most mainline churches have avoided calling for removal of programs they find offensive. However, others, equating "tolerance for" with "acceptance of," would, indeed, banish programs they consider sacrilegious or that portray lifestyles and behaviors they find reprehensible.

In spite of differences in approach to what they see as the problem of inappropriate content, all churches, believing they have the truth, easily forget that the same First Amendment that protects their religion and their right to criticize also protects those holding different understandings of God and his commands.

Good and faithful Christians differ in regard to what they believe is acceptable programming, even as Christians differ from Jews, Muslims, Hindus, and the myriad others who make up the American mosaic. As cultural shifts from the McCarthy era to the era of civil rights demonstrations, antiwar protests, and the counterculture of the 1960s and early 1970s and then to an era of contracts "with America" and "for the American family" suggest, one era's "moral majority" can quickly become a "deviant minority." Thus, just as media professionals need to be sensitive both to the concerns of religious people and to shifts in the cultural climate, religious people must be sensitive to the demands of a pluralistic society. In such a society, they must expect and protect attacks, criticism, voicing of concerns, and portrayals of behaviors they find inimical to true religion as they understand it, if they are to see their own freedom of belief and expression protected when cultural winds again shift.

While some would say that only the government can censor, any group with sufficient resources can stop the transmission or publication of matter considered objectionable. In seeking for their own purposes, however nobly intended, control over "reality definition," it is apparent that in America, church leaders across the religious spectrum could easily become: "a very able cadre of American Ayatollahs who are going to do this country in [in] the way the Ayatollah Khomeini is doing Iran in, if we're not very careful."[21]

NOTES

This research was conducted as a service learning project on behalf of the First Amendment Congress of Denver, Colorado. The author thanks Jean Otto, President, and Julie Lucas, Executive Director of the Congress, for their support.

1. George Gallup, Jr., and Frank Newport, "Americans Have Love-Hate Relationship with Their TV sets," *The Gallup Poll Monthly* (October, 1990), pp. 2-14.

2. But see Eve Pell, *The Big Chill: How the Reagan Administration, Corporate America, and Religious Conservatives Are Subverting Free Speech and the Public's Right to Know* (Boston: Beacon Press, 1984), pp. 98-106.

3. See William Noble, *Bookbanning in America: Who Bans Books?—and Why* (Middlebury, VT: Paul S. Eriksson, 1960); E. M. Oboler, *The Fear of the Word: Censorship and Sex* (Metuchen, NJ: The Scarecrow Press, 1974); Sue Curry Jansen, *Censorship: The Knot that Binds Power and Knowledge* (New York: Oxford University Press, 1991); Marjorie Heins, *Sin, Sex, and Blasphemy: A Guide to America's Censorship Wars* (New York: The New Press, 1993); George Beahm, ed., *War of Words: The Censorship Debate* (Kansas City, MO: Andrews and McMeel, 1993); Thomas R. Lindlof, "The Passionate Audience: Community Inscriptions of 'The Last Temptation of Christ,' " in Daniel A. Stout and Judith M. Buddenbaum, eds., *Religion and Mass Media: Audiences and Adaptations* (Thousand Oaks, CA: Sage, 1996), pp. 148-168.

4. James Davison Hunter, *Culture Wars: The Struggle to Define America* (New York: Basic Books, 1991); see also Marvin Olasky, *The Prodigal Press: The Anti-Christian Bias of the American News Media* (Westchester, IL: Crossway Books, 1988).

5. Nancy Signorelli and Michael Morgan, eds., *Cultivation Analysis: New Directions in Media Effects Research* (Newbury Park, CA: Sage, 1990).

6. David L. Protess and Maxwell McCombs, eds., *Agenda Setting: Readings on Media, Public Opinion, and Policymaking* (Hillsdale, NJ: Lawrence Erlbaum Associates, 1991).

7. Hunter, *Culture Wars.*

8. Gerhard Lenski, *The Religious Factor* (Garden City, NY: Doubleday, 1963); Samuel A. Stouffer, *Communism, Conformity, and Civil Liberties* (Gloucester, MA: Peter Smith, 1963); Clyde Z. Nunn, Harry J. Crockett, and J. Allen Williams, Jr., *Tolerance for Nonconformity: A National Survey of Americans' Changing Commitment to Civil Liberties* (San Francisco: Jossey-Bass, 1978); Michael Corbett, *Political Tolerance in America: Freedom and Equality in Public Attitudes* (New York: Longman, 1982); Karen von Elten and Tony Rimmer, "Television and Newspaper Reliance and Tolerance for Civil Liberties," *Mass Communication Review* 19 (1992), pp. 27-35; Tony Rimmer, "Religion, Mass Media and Tolerance for Civil Liberties," in Stout and Buddenbaum, *Religion and Mass Media*, pp. 105-122.

9. Robert Wuthnow, *The Struggle for America's Soul: Evangelicals, Liberals and Secularism* (Grand Rapids, MI: Wm. B. Eerdmans, 1989).

10. Kenneth B. Bedell, *Yearbook of American and Canadian Churches* (Nashville, TN: Abingdon Press, 1993).

11. Questions about support for expressive rights were selected primarily to reflect students' interests. To facilitate comparison between clergy responses and those from a national sample of the general public, both questions and response options were taken from a study by Wyatt (Robert O. Wyatt, *Free Expression and the American Public: A Survey Commemorating the 200th Anniversary of the First Amendment* [Murfreesboro, TN: Middle Tennessee State University, 1991]), even though the "never, sometimes, always" categories make judgments about degree of support somewhat problematic.

While one can safely conclude that those who chose the "never protected" option are less protective of a particular kind of expression than those who chose "sometimes protected" or "always protected," differences in support between those who chose "sometimes" and those who chose "always" are less clear. Clergy who chose "sometimes" for all or most kinds of expression may have been thinking less in terms of the content than in the appropriateness of "time, place, and manner" restrictions which, according to current court interpretation, are not considered abridgments of First Amendment rights so long as they serve a serious government purpose, are content neutral, and do not block all avenues for expression of otherwise protected speech.

Although all of the kinds of expression included in this study have been judged protected under the First Amendment, speech offending others because of their religion might be punishable as "fighting words" if it were directly and personally addressed so the speech becomes the verbal equivalent of the first blow in a fight. Mere nudity, portrayals of homosexuality, and movies that are rated as suitable only for an adult audience because of sexual content do not meet current legal definitions for obscene, and therefore unprotected, speech. However, nudity, some portrayals of homosexuality, and some adult movies might very well be indecent or even obscene according to current interpretations of the Federal Communication Act's proscription against "profane, indecent and obscene" content. Thus some might have to be channeled to late at night if they were judged indecent by broadcast standards, or, if obscene by broadcast standards, completely banished from VHF and UHF television stations, but not necessarily from cable stations, especially if they were shown on cable channels provided as add-ons to basic service.

12. Roger Finke and Rodney Stark, *The Churching of America 1776-1990: Winners and Losers in Our Religious Economy* (New Brunswick, NJ: Rutgers University Press, 1992), pp. 16-22.

13. Wade Clark Roof and William C. McKinney, *American Mainline Religion: Its Changing Shape and Future* (New Brunswick, NJ: Rutgers University Press, 1987); Barry A. Kosmin and Seymour P. Lachman, *One Nation Under God: Religion in Contemporary American Society* (New York: Harmony Books, 1993).

14. See Jennings Bryant and Dolph Zillmann, *Perspectives on Media Effects* (Hillsdale, NJ: Lawrence Erlbaum Associates, 1986); Signorelli and Morgan, *Cultivation Analysis*; Protess and McCombs, *Agenda Setting.*

15. Churchill L. Roberts, "Attitudes and Media Use of the Moral Majority," *Journal of Broadcasting* 27 (Fall, 1983), pp. 403-410; Neal F. Hamilton and Alan M. Rubin, "The Influence of Religiosity on Television Viewing," *Journalism Quarterly* 69 (Fall, 1992), pp. 667-678; JoAnn Myer Valenti and Daniel A. Stout, "Diversity from Within: An Analysis of the Impact of Religious Culture on Media Use and Effective Communication to Women," in Stout and Buddenbaum, *Religion and Mass Media*, pp. 183-196.

16. John Stuart Mill, *On Liberty* (Indianapolis, IN: Bobbs-Merrill, 1956).

17. John Milton, "Aereopagitica," in John Patrick, ed., *The Prose of John Milton* (New York: New York University Press, 1968), pp. 326-345.

18. See James W. Skillen, *The Scattered Voice: Christians at Odds in the Public Square* (Grand Rapids, MI: Zondervan Books, 1990); Stout and Buddenbaum, *Religion and Mass Media.*

19. Lee C. Bollinger, *The Tolerant Society* (New York: Oxford University Press, 1986).

20. See William F. Fore, *Mythmakers: Gospel, Culture and the Media* (New York: Friendship Press, 1990); National Council of Churches, *Global Communication for Justice* (New York: National Council of Churches in Christ, 1992); National Council of Churches, "Violence in the Electronic Media," Nov. 11, 1993, a policy statement adopted by the General Board, National Council of Churches in Christ.

21. James Michener, "Are There Limits to Free Speech?" in Beahm, *War of Words*, pp. 20-24.

10

Blurred Boundaries: Religion and Prime Time Television

Wade Clark Roof

Making sense of life in a fast-paced, uncertain world is a challenge. In a recent nationwide survey, almost two-thirds (64%) of adult Americans complained that "life is too complex these days"—a response even more telling considering that these same people also believe that the future will be more fast-paced and more uncertain.[1] They feel that they are being left behind, that social and technological change threatens to undo them. The result is information overload, psychological dissonance, saturated selves, to cite the usual alarms. George Barna, who conducted the survey, writes: "we are drowning in the sea of breakthroughs and transformations that have already been left behind in our society's unending quest for progress."[2]

The sources of this malaise in contemporary America are numerous, but clearly the media industries figure into it. Never before has human life been so shaped by mediated image and symbol. And never before have people been so aware that ours is a world caught up in image and symbol. Increasingly, ours is a self-reflexive world in which people ponder the meanings of their lives in a context of seeming flux and impermanence. Taste, preference, hyperreality, generic culture, style, consumption—all are a production of the media, and all convey a reality in marked contrast to what we have known in the past. This gap between the way we are and the way we were, or imagine we were, seems to intensify, but even this is bound up closely with the media and its powers at shaping our imageries. *Image and narrative*—historically very much related to religion—are more and more in the media's control. And consequently, the boundaries between religion and the media, I believe, are becoming blurred. If this is true, then we now confront a new set of institutional dynamics in the late twentieth century, a challenge for all of us, television producers and executives, religionists, and concerned citizens alike.

Several features of our religious situation today seem unmistakable, though it is far easier to identify them than to fully account for them. Here I identify briefly three such features.

One such trend is the erosion of authority and influence of religious institutions. It is a trend long underway but is increasingly apparent in our time. I refer to a loss of power on the part of religious leaders to compel action and thereby influence popular opinion and values. While this loss of power is generally understood, what is not always so well known is the larger context in which it has occurred. More than just increased competition from other organizations or estrangement of the laity from religious institutions, religious elites are increasingly marginalized through structural displacement, owing to the rise of large-scale capitalism, the nation-state, and large bureaucracies. Influence has shifted from the religious sphere to the economic, political, and cultural-production industries. Compared to these larger structures of cultural power, traditional religious institutions now lack especially, as James Davidson Hunter and James E. Howland write, "the power to create and maintain a definition of public reality."[3]

A second feature is the increased role of the media industries in the contemporary matrix of institutions. This is widely recognized as well, but it too is not fully appreciated. Just as the printing press over four hundred years ago changed communication and the structures through which discourse occurs, so more recent advances in media technology have greatly transformed the way we know and what we know. Put simply, the power to define "the public sphere" and to control access to its discourse is now largely under the control of the media and related cultural industries. Visual media and global networks have added to this power and control. It might be said that modernity has created a context in which definitions of reality and even the philosophical foundations on which society itself rests are themselves now questioned, which means that the symbolic frames produced by the media take on even greater significance. The profile of culture increases in an age when we are more aware than ever that images, values, signs, even metaphysical assertions, are consciously produced, and when societal values and moral presuppositions are hotly debated—a situation that once led Baudrillard to comment, somewhat glibly, that everything today is cultural.[4]

A third feature is the greater personal autonomy people assume in matters of religious faith and practice. Americans increasingly *choose* whether to believe and what to believe with regard to the sacred. People switch from one faith to another with relative ease; they move in and out of religious organizations during the life span. Often they drop out of churches and synagogues but still claim to be good Catholics, Protestants, Jews, or whatever. They mix elements from a variety of traditions such as Native American teachings, ecology, feminism, psychotherapy, Christianity, psychology, and science, creating what Canadian sociologist Reginald Bibby calls "religion a la carte."[5] Everywhere on the contemporary religious landscape, it seems, there are signs of an expanding culture of choice. This exaltation of the individual's own authority to make religious decisions has come about just when authority within religious institutions has eroded. It might be said that the strong hold of ascriptive social factors (e.g., the social class or ethnicity a person is born into) upon people's lives has lost force, or as Peter Berger is fond of saying, modernity has brought about a psychological shift "from fate to choice."[6]

What then are we to make of these big trends? How do they impact upon prime time television? Mass media theorist Stewart M. Hoover puts forth a compelling thesis. He argues that in this changing context the media industries "now define and condition access to the public sphere in a way that cannot be escaped by any social institution."[7] His is a persuasive argument, and one we cannot dismiss as it applies to religion.

When Hoover says that no institution can now escape the impact of the media industries, he has in mind how the latter transforms all patterns of communication. He speaks of the media industries as "overtaking" other institutions in the sense that they set the terms for how they relate to one another. To appreciate how this occurs, he identifies three types or contexts of communication: (1) *private* communication, as occurs in a close-bounded setting where people know one another and share values and beliefs; (2) *community* communication, as occurs within a collectivity such as a church, temple, or mosque where the values, beliefs, and moral discourse arise out of a historic tradition; and (3) *public* communication, as occurs in a more open setting such as lectures, publications, and visual media. It is this latter type of communication, now in an age of media industries, that "overtakes" all other types of communication.

This means that public communication—not the discourse of religious communities—controls the public sphere, and thereby defines the meaning-contexts in which other types of communication take place. Not only do the media industries shape interpretation, they encourage the privatization of religious meanings and values. Whereas in a more "organic" era of the past, Hoover argues, community-level consciousness and action might have had considerable space and scope, now "community is constrained by the demands to accommodate to either a wholly private realm of individual action or to a public realm of discourse. Religious movements and religious institutions, which once existed quite comfortably in that 'middle,' are now forced in either of these directions."[8] Thus for religion's role in society, the impact of the media becomes crucial. For if it is true as some now say that we "live in" communication, then it is the case that religious language contains its greatest meaning and will have most influence either in the context of individuals communicating with one another, presumably in a face-to-face situation, or in a reformulated mode of discourse shaped by the mediated public realm. Either way, a major structural shift in religion's relation to the modern order has occurred, with major implications for the practice and expression of religious beliefs and values within society.

This being the case, we can rightly think of religion as facing a new set of conditions. Both the meaning of religious discourse and its institutional locus are in the balance. What does this mean for religion on prime time television?

Perhaps the most significant implication is, as Hoover says, that religion "must exist in *public*, and that means in the media."[9] Practically speaking, this means two things: one, religious discourse is "flattened" to fit the public realm, and, two, the meaning of religion is shaped in keeping with particular categories of interpretation. "Flattening" here refers to a process of civilizing faith, of softening it, making it non-offensive. A case in point is evangelicalism. Here pressures have clearly mounted over the past two decades toward flattening, a deemphasis of the more offensive elements of evangelical tradition (e.g., belief in hell, the wrath of God, sin) along with a posturing by evangelical leaders and media consultants to make the tradition more acceptable in a context of cultural plurality. Commenting on this shift in stylization, James Davidson Hunter writes: "This has entailed a softening and a polishing of the more hardline and barbed elements of the orthodox Protestant world view. Although at its doctrinal core this world view remains essentially unchanged, it has been culturally edited to give it the qualities of sociability and gentility. It has acquired a civility that proclaims loudly, 'No offense, I am an Evangelical.' "[10] This shift in stylization leads to religious interpretation using current cultural categories. Such categories come into play as "experience," "self-fulfillment," "emotional maturity," and "psychological balance"—all reflecting a post-1960s, subjective culture. Preoccupation with the self is a dominant motif. It is a mode of religious discourse that appeals to an empty or depleted self. It is a mode of discourse that presumes, and also greatly reinforces, a view of religious symbols and meaning as limited to the private sphere.

Both processes—flattening and reinterpreting—contribute to the blurring of boundaries. Religions—except for "cults"—begin to look more like one another as they become tamed through television. And as faith is recast in psychological categories, it becomes another of media's many "symbolic repertoires," each somehow different yet not too different. Faith is happiness, fulfillment, contentment, identifiable as something distinctly spiritual but similar to the benefits people obtain from the soaps and talk shows.

The media's role in defining religious symbols and meanings raises another serious consideration: who has access to the public sphere? That becomes more and more important not just because of the dominance of public communication but because of the spiraling costs of media technology and air time. Prior to the 1960s religious broadcasting was regarded as public service broadcasting, but beginning in that decade the Federal Communications Commission opened the door to free-market principles of religious broadcasting.[11] The advent of videotape technology during this same period made it possible to air the same program in hundreds of cities simultaneously. Taken together, these developments had far-reaching consequences for religion: simply put, they had the effect of making air time open only to those who could pay top dollar for it. And from the 1970s to the present, conservative, evangelical Protestant constituencies have voted with their dollars by purchasing air time, far more so than either mainline Protestants, Catholics, or Jews. It is said that religious developments in the United States often lend themselves to "supply side" interpretation, and here we see a clear instance of how those able and willing to mobilize resources are then in a position to exercise influence: money is translated into control over the airwaves, and hence into power to shape faith, including its moral and political meanings, and to confront secular culture.

Again, the stage is set for blurred boundaries. Caught in the grip of capitalism, television becomes a functional extension of the church, or better put, of the church that can pay. At least television should be a carrier of wholesome, if not distinctly religious, values—so goes the argument of many conservatives and moderates alike. And if it does not do this, then what happens in the prime time hours is subject to normative censorship. Boycotts against sponsors of network or local television stations because of their choice of programming content (pertaining to abortion, explicit sex, and "family values") in prime time hours taps strong moral and religious sentiments and a sense that the values that the offended viewers hold dearly are not being ritually affirmed.[12] For many television watchers, this amounts to a serious offense and a further blurring of the lines between religion and entertainment.

Still another case—and the extreme case of blurred boundaries—emerges when religious meanings and values find expression in secular programming. The media encourage a sense of personal identity that is reflexive, that is, a conception of self as constructed and seemingly more open and protean. But a paradox arises: on the one hand, visual media contribute to a more fluid self, yet on the other hand, it attempts to structure an identity amidst the flux. This "new" identity is one which recognizes and accepts choice, and maybe even some degree of instability. Within television, as Douglas Kellner says, identity becomes largely a "theatrical presentation of self, in which one is able to present oneself in a variety of roles, images, and activities, relatively unconcerned about shifts, transformations, and dramatic changes."[13] Perhaps this is an overstatement, yet he captures something of the changes in identity and self-conceptions now occurring.

With regard to religion, this more fluid self is both a bane and a blessing. At one level, television operates in a context that encourages "religion a la carte," cafeteria religion, pastiche, bricolage, to list a few labels now in vogue. People are presented with a menu of religious and spiritual themes, and they are put in the position of picking and choosing among them, or of mixing elements eclectically. Experience is privileged over belief, exploration takes precedence over certitude; coherence and inner meaning are more important than rational consistency. Television is not to be blamed for all of modernity's ills, but it must accept its share of responsibility for creating a world where individuals are less rooted in traditions and are becoming, as Zygmunt Bauman says, more like tourists in relation to the sacred than like believers.[14]

Yet it is also the case that television is engaged in an identity-formation process, and one in which religious and spiritual themes can and often do surface. Programs like "Northern Exposure," "Picket Fences," "ER," and "Chicago Hope" present audiences with existential encounters arising out of everyday life and which have the potential for provoking religious or mystical-spiritual responses. Examples would include such moments as whether to pull the plug on an aging spouse, the discovery of one's deeper self in love and relationships, finding that faith has layers of meaning that one has forgotten or repressed, and celebration of one's spiritual relationship to the earth. "Journey" and "recovery" themes are widely celebrated in keeping with historic motifs of pilgrimage, healing, visualization, ancient wisdom, and self-actualization. All are motifs prominent in the popular culture, especially for generations born after World War II; baby boomers and Generation Xers, who have weaker ties to organized religion than do older Americans, comprise a large market for spiritual exploration.[15]

In this respect television assumes some of the functions traditionally ascribed to religious myth and ritual. But it does so in ways that are subtle and by means of vocabularies that are at best quasi-religious. Even aspects of religious community are involved—"communities of interpretation" where people share, to some degree, a common vocabulary concerning such things as spiritual quest and self-discovery.[16] Seldom is religion dealt with as an integrated set of religious beliefs, values, and symbols—that is, as inherited tradition—but is framed more as a moment or encounter arising out of personal experience or crisis. Another difference is that the television audience is presented with only fleeting insights—glimpses really—into life, healing, spiritual depth, transcendence; those watching can make of these epiphanies what they please since an explicit religious script is not provided. Television's images and narratives contain multiple encodings and decodings, which makes for extended interpretation—religious or otherwise—by the self-reflecting individual.

This blurring of boundaries between religion and the media occurs today in a broadly based, rapidly changing institutional matrix. Perhaps we stand too close to all of this to grasp fully what is happening, much less to have a vision of where it leads for the future. On reflection, we recognize that religion is incredibly complex: what it is, how and where it gets expressed, the contexts of its meanings, are all more complicated than we might at first imagine. And today certainly, all of these are issues for debate as they bear upon prime time television and its role with respect to popular values.

By design or not, television programming forces upon audiences enormous responsibility. Individuals have to make choices about the quality and suitability of the programs they watch; they must take the lead in constructing any religious or spiritual meaning that might possibly be derived from the programs. It is also clear that Americans are increasingly calling for the television industry to be more responsible, particularly in regard to values, moral sensibilities, and in its appeal to the human spirit. And if the trends we have identified in this paper are correct, such concerns will not soon go away. Emile Durkheim, the great French sociologist, observed how religion is deeply intertwined in the ritual affirmations of society itself; the media are now a part of that ritual process and must, therefore, face the pressures of a concerned public.

NOTES

1. George Barna, *Virtual America* (Ventura: Regal Books, 1994), p. 79.

2. Barna, *Virtual America,* p. 79.

3. James Davidson Hunter and James E. Hawdon, "Religious Elites in Advanced Capitalism: The Dialectic of Power and Marginality," in Wade Clark Roof, ed., *World Order and Religion* (Albany: SUNY Press, 1991), p. 40.

4. J. Baudrillard, *In the Shadow of the Silent Majorities* (New York: Semiotext, 1983).

5. Reginald Bibby, *Fragmented Gods: The Poverty and Potential of Religion in Canada* (Toronto: Irwin, 1987).

6. Peter L. Berger, *The Heretical Imperative* (New York: Doubleday, 1980).

7. Stewart M. Hoover, "Mass Media and Religious Pluralism," in Philip Lee, ed., *The Democratization of Communication* (Cardiff: University of Wales Press, 1996).

8. Hoover, "Mass Media and Religious Pluralism."

9. Hoover, "Mass Media and Religious Pluralism."

10. James Davidson Hunter, *American Evangelicalism: Conservative Religion and the Quandary of Modernity* (New Brunswick, NJ: Rutgers University Press, 1983).

11. See Jeffrey K. Hadden, "The Rise and Fall of American Televangelism," *The Annals of the American Academy of Political and Social Science* 527 (May 1993), pp. 113-130.

12. See *Los Angeles Times*, October 15, 1995, front page story "Racy Programs Creeping into Family Hour."

13. Douglas Kellner, "Popular Culture and the Construction of Post-Modern Identities," in Scott Lash and Jonathan Friedman (eds.), *Modernity and Identity* (Oxford: Blackwell Publishers, 1992), p. 158.

14. Zygmunt Bauman, *Life in Fragments: Essays in Postmodern Morality* (Oxford: Blackwell Publishers, 1995).

15. Wade Clark Roof, *A Generation of Seekers* (San Francisco: HarperCollins, 1993).

16. John Fiske, *Television Culture* (London: Routledge, 1987).

11

Do We Really Need More Religion on Fiction Television?

Michael Suman

Does religion get a fair shake on entertainment television? Critics argue that there is not enough religion on fiction television and that portrayals of religious life that do make their way onto the tube are too often disrespectful and negative. Television constitutes an important part of the public square. An essential aspect of the religion-on-television debate is what place or role religion in general should have in the American public square. Throughout the history of the United States, many Americans have recognized the dangers involved in giving religion too central a place in public life. Before rushing to fill prime time with preachers, priests, and piety, we should pause to consider these perennial concerns.

A *U.S. News and World Report* poll published in April 1994 reported on the state of religion in America. One of the major findings was that though Americans, on the whole, are a very religious people and consider religion to be a very important part of their private lives, they are wary of religion playing too prominent a role in the public square. The article cited "the perpetual tension between our religious impulses and our unwavering commitment to a secular society." It noted that "[w]e want our leaders to adhere to spiritual values yet are suspicious of politicians who seem too eager to appropriate the trappings and jargon of faith."[1] Stephen Carter, in his much discussed *The Culture of Disbelief*, noted the same tension. "We are one of the most religious nations on earth, in the sense that we have a deeply religious citizenry; but we are also perhaps the most zealous in guarding our public institutions against explicit religious influences."[2]

Carter goes on to argue that, despite this tension, religion should play a much larger role in public life. In this, current critics who argue that religion on television is too often belittled and, more frequently, ignored would concur. They hold that in this realm of public life, religion should be much more conspicuous, especially positive portrayals of religious life. But is this really such a good idea? Do we have anything to fear from a more prominent role of religion in the public square, particularly in the realm of entertainment television? Why shouldn't all Amercans rush to embrace this larger role for religion in public life?

American discomfort with too much religion in the public square is rooted in historical realities. Of particular relevance here is the pluralistic nature of the American religious landscape and the related religious intolerance and bigotry that have been directed by majority groups against minority groups thoughout American history. To understand the current debate, these historical realities of religiously pluralistic America must be explored.

One of our cherished cultural traditions is that America has served as a haven for those suffering religious persecution elsewhere. In fact, many of the original colonists left the old world to escape religious tyranny. This resulted in a colonial America in which religious pluralism was rampant. But this is not to say that all of these religious groups co-existed in harmony. In fact, most of the colonies (nine of the thirteen) established their own churches and persecuted, to one degree or another, those who worshipped and believed differently.

Although religious liberty was one of the goals of many early immigrants, many of the religious tyrannies of the old world were carried over into the new. Persons who dissented were often expelled from a colony or, if allowed to stay, accorded, at best, second class citizenship. Quakers, Baptists, and Anglicans were banished from some of the New England colonies. Jews were expelled from New York, Huguenots from Florida, and Catholics from almost everywhere except Maryland.[3] In Massachusetts colonial law compelled everyone to attend religious services, regardless of personal beliefs. Laws stipulated that any Quakers, "that cursed sect of heretics," who entered the colony were to be jailed, whipped with twenty stripes, and then expelled. Some Quakers were branded. Others had their ears cut off. Four were hanged. In at least one case the children of Quakers, upon authorization of a Boston court, were sold into slavery. The Quakers also had a hard time in Virginia where law designated them as "an unreasonable and turbulent sort of people . . . teaching and publishing lies, miracles, false visions, prophecies, and doctrines."[4] In Virginia all citizens were taxed to support the Anglican church, the services of which they were required to attend each week. Early Virginia laws held that anyone convicted a third time for failure to attend religious services was to spend six months in the galleys. No non-Anglican group was allowed to hold services. No non-Anglican could hold public office. Belief in infant baptism was a requirement for citizenship. Blasphemy, impious references to the Trinity, habitual cursing, and a third offense of working on the sabbath were all punishable by death.[5] Many of the colonies had religious tests for holding office. Maryland required that an officer profess "belief in the Christian religion," North Carolina that one profess the "divine authority" of the Bible, Pennsylvania that one "confess a belief in God."[6]

In these early days religious hostilities were ubiquitous and peace among the different groups was often thought to be an impossibility.[7] This aspect of our historical record should give us pause. Religious persecution and intolerance are not solely foreign products. Fortunately, America moved beyond this particular set of circumstances.

Gradually this situation changed as increasing tolerance was recognized as a necessity if peace and order were to prevail. To a significant extent this occurred because there were so many different religious groups. The colonies and, subsequently, states became home to increasing numbers of dissenters and minority religious group members. It was not that the particular groups did not want to retain their privileged status. Rather, it was a matter of their no longer having dominant majorities. Moreover, the early pattern of state churches and their intolerance was repudiated in the First Amendment. However one interprets the First Amendment, the framers clearly sought religious freedom for all. Similarly, Jefferson wrote that his Virginia Statute for Religious Freedom was "to comprehend within the mantle of its protection the Jew and Gentile, the Christian and Mahometan, the Hindoo, and infidel of every denomination." He later commented that he did not care if his neighbors believed in one god or twenty, so long as they kept the civil peace.[8]

By placing no restrictions on the free exercise of religion and by refraining from giving preferential status to any particular religion, the framers virtually ensured the continuance and flourishing of America's religious pluralism. By the 1830s the legal framework of disestablishment and religious free exercise was well in place, and hundreds, if not thousands, of religious groups exploded onto the American scene.

The religious arrangement created in early nineteenth century America was a vast improvement over the conflict-ridden situation of colonial America, but this did not mean that religious intolerance ended. Though clearly a religiously pluralistic nation, America was one with a decided Christian bias. This bias was exemplified in the Girard case of 1844. In 1831, Stephen Girard provided in his will for the establishment of a college for orphans, but he stipulated a condition. Although the orphans were to be taught the "purest principles of morality," no clergy members representing any religion whatsoever were to teach at, hold office in, or even visit the proposed school. Upon challenge of the will, the Supreme Court ruled that Girard's conditions referred to clergy, but certainly not to Christianity itself. Regarding the requirement that teachers in the school "instill into the minds of the scholars the purest principles of morality" the Court commented: "Where can the purest principles of morality be learned so clearly or so perfectly as from the New Testament?"[9]

The bias was not only Christian, it was also decidedly Protestant. (Of the approximately four and a half million citizens in America in 1766, only about twenty thousand were Catholic.) The non-official establishment of a Protestant Christian hegemony undoubtedly was a major reason why citizens accepted the radically new concept of separation of church and state enunciated in the First Amendment. The challenging of this Protestant Christian dominance by waves of Catholic and Jewish immigrants in the nineteeth and early twentieth centuries was met with virulent bigotry and discrimination against these groups. As Catholics flowed into the country there were numerous attempts to amend immigration laws to stem the flow. Barring that, there were strenuous efforts to convert them to Protestantism. The Know-Nothing political party was formed with anti-Catholicism as one of its unifying themes. Countless laws were passed in state legislatures specifically directed against Catholic immigrants. Propagandists warned of Papist plots to take over the country. There were riots in which Catholic churches were destroyed, Catholic homes were burned, and Catholics were killed. Other groups outside of the Protestant mainstream sufferred similar fates. The Ku Klux Klan made antisemitism one of its major tenets. The Mormons were successively run out of New York, Ohio, Missouri, and Illinois before finally securing a relatively uninhabited region of Utah. From their beginnings, the Jehovah's Witnesses were subject to ridicule and persecution.[10]

Protestant Christian domination has continued well into the twentieth century. Robert Handy has argued that Protestants maintained a de facto establishment in American life until after World War II.[11] Nevertheless, in some ways Protestant America grew more comfortable with non-Protestant groups that share the Judeo-Christian tradition. The post-World War II additions of "In God We Trust" on our money and "under God" in the Pledge of Allegiance are inclusive in this regard. But this has certainly not spelled an end to religious intolerance and bigotry. With this in mind, let us look at the comtemporary scene.

One of the most significant developments of the last twenty-five years has been the arrival to the United States of many adherents of Eastern and Middle-Eastern religions, especially Muslims, Buddhists, and Hindus. By some estimates, there are now over six million Muslims, three million Hindus, and three million Buddhists in the United States.[12] Precise numbers are debatable and these estimates are most likely high, but the fact that each of these groups is sizable and has growth rates that are among the highest in the country is not. These religions, which on many issues provide stark alternatives to Christianity, are supported by sizable and growing immigrant communities that are confronting Judeo-Christian America. America has also witnessed the growth of New Thought metaphysical churches, occult religions, spiritualism, theosophy, and astrology. Native American Indian religious traditions have also undergone a revival. Here we can also add the development of the quasi-religious therapeutic movement, including such things as the booming twelve-step programs. Terry Muck in *Alien Gods on American Turf* states that of the approximately 1,500 religious groups in the U.S., 600 are non-Christian.[13] Of course the Christian community continues to dominate the American scene. Derek Davis estimates that Protestants now constitute about 35% of the total population and Catholics about 24%, together constituting a Christian majority. Jews constitute another 2-1/2%. But this leaves a very significant proportion of the American community outside of the Judeo-Christian tradition.[14] We can quibble over precise numbers and percentages (Davis probably underestimates the size of the Judeo-Christian majority), but the fact remains that the United States is now the most religiously pluralistic nation in the world, and it is becoming more so. And this pluralism is lessening the dominance of the Judeo-Christian tradition.

The increase in pluralism is not the only change in the contemporary American religious scene. Robert Wuthnow has discussed a restructuring of American religion. He includes in this restructuring the boom in pluralism discussed above. He also describes the decline in importance of formal religious institutions, manifested in terms of decline in denominational loyalty, decline in the political and cultural prominence of the traditional religious bodies, and decline in the over-all legitimacy of those bodies. Replacing faith and loyalty to established religious institutions has been an increasing personal autonomy in matters of faith. As institutional claims and loyalties hold less power over individuals, they consider themselves to be the final authority over the nature and relevance of their faith. In other words, people are taking matters of faith into their own hands. Matters of faith and belief revolve more around the self than the group. Religion becomes increasingly subjective and private, focused inward toward one's own unique spiritual journey and meeting one's own personal needs.[15] The aforementioned *U.S. News* poll noted this "growing trend toward self-focused religion and a 'spirituality turned inward.' "[16] Often this orientation involves crafting one's own religious beliefs and values by picking and choosing cafeteria style from the range of those which are culturally available. In *Habits of the Heart*, Robert Bellah et al. refer to this orientation as "Sheila-ism," after a woman who named her religion after herself. The authors suggested that this makes for the logical possibility of over two hundred million different religions in the United States.[17] Pluralism indeed.[18]

(This personalization and privatization of religion is consistent with the general understanding of secularization outlined by Talcott Parsons. As commonly understood, secularization refers to the displacement of religious interpretations of reality and religious orientations toward life by an orientation that seeks explanations for and justifications of human behavior and other phenomena in rational and scientific terms. A second understanding proposed by Parsons refers to a process of increasing differentiation between the religious and secular [non-religious] spheres of life. This process coincides with and perhaps results from increasing specialization in society as it industrializes and becomes more modern and urban.[19] Similarly Max Weber argued that with modernity and industrialization scientific rationality begins to displace religious orientations to the world. One possibility for religious belief systems, according to Weber, is to move ever more exclusively into the private sphere and out of the public sphere, which is increasingly dominated by rationalist discourse.[20])

What response has Christian America given to this increasing religious pluralism and increasing personalization and privatization of religion? One response has been the old religious intolerance and bigotry. Among some Christians there has been a call for a return to "Christian America." Sessions of a conservative Christian forum held in Memphis in January 1996, entitled the "National Affairs Briefing," began with a Christian version of the Pledge of Allegiance which begins, "I pledge allegiance to the Christian flag and to the Savior for whose Kingdom it stands."[21] Threatened by the loss of Christian hegemony, the call is "Take America Back!" This slogan, popular among religious conservatives, can be found on everything from return address labels to T-shirts.[22] It was a popular item in the latter form at a three-day conference held in Florida in March 1996. The conference was entitled "Reclaiming America for Christ." Along the same lines, in early April 1995 Pat Robertson, on the "700 Club," said of Hinduism, "We can't let this kind of thing come into America." When a Muslim cleric was invited to give the daily prayer in Congress, Robertson asked if now the door would be opened to "all kinds of weirdness."[23] Similarly, David Wardell, co-founder and ambassador-at-large of Promise Keepers, has blamed many of America's problems on the breakdown of the Protestant Christian hegemony. He points to "all these foreign religions and a countless myriad of beliefs without unity."[24]

One of these elements that seeks to recapture America for Christianity is the Christian Reconstructionist movement which proposes installing a political system in America based entirely on biblical law. Rousas Rushdoony, a leading Reconstructionist, envisions a society in which no faith other than Christianity would be tolerated. All heresy would be stamped out through the civil enforcement of biblical law. The Reconstruction movement claims twenty million members, but it is no doubt considerably smaller.

A much more populous movement calling for a return to a Christian America is the religious or Christian right. Many members of this group also seek a form of theocracy. A February 1997 Gallup poll of members of the Christian right sponsored by the American Jewish Committee found that 48% think that a constitutional amendment should be adopted "declaring the United States a Christian nation." But the version of theocracy that this group is after is considerably milder than that sought by the Reconstructionists. Jerry Falwell asserts that "God promoted America to a greatness no other nation has ever enjoyed because her heritage is one of a republic governed by laws predicated on the Bible." He adds that "America's future depends on her accepting and demonstrating God's government."[25] Pat Robertson's "grand plan" is essentially a call for an American Protestant theocracy. He denies that there should be separation of church and state. "The radical left has kept us in submission because they have talked about separation of church and state," Robertson says. "There is no such thing in the Constitution. It's a lie of the left, and we're not going to take it anymore." As for the Constitution, Robertson argues that it "is a marvelous document for self-government for Christian people, but the minute you turn the document into the hands of non-Christians and atheist people, they can use it to destroy the very foundation of our society." When he ran for president, he formulated an explicit religious test for public office, stating repeatedly that he would not consider appointing any Muslims or Hindus to his cabinet.[26]

For the most part, the leaders of the religious right call not so much for enactment of biblical law as for a thorough infusion of Christian principles into the way the country operates. Note Pat Buchanan's call for a Christian jihad, a holy war for Christian values. David Barton, in *The Myth of Separation*, argues that this is what the Founding Fathers had in mind. They intended that the United States should be a Christian nation, not because it was populated exclusively by Christians, but because it was founded upon and would be governed according to Christian principles.[27] It seems that according to the basic program of the Christian right, American law would become Christianized and non-believers would, over time, become convinced of the merits of this. As Derek Davis describes it, "Non-Christians would not be denied the right to worship privately according to their own beliefs, but they would be expected to submit to a public agenda that implemented Christian ideals in many quarters. There would be Christian prayer in public schools, Christian symbols in the public square, public monies available to religious enterprises (with most going to the majority and culturally dominant faith, Christianity), and governments in which the principal seats were held by Christians."[28] In other words, the basic goal is reformation of the civil order, with Christian values and beliefs imposed on society, through force of law if necessary.

Members of the Christian right are not comfortable with a nation that is becoming increasingly more pluralistic. They are not comfortable with cafeteria-style Christians who pick and choose what they like about Christianity, as well as other faiths, to incorporate into their own personal religions (Sheilas). They are not comfortable with atheists and non-believers, whom Pat Buchanan lumps together with "flag burners, illegal aliens—including terrorists—convicts and pornographers."[29] They are not comfortable with any non-Judeo-Christian religions. A 1995 survey reveals that half of "born-again Christians" (a category including members of the Christian right but also including some less conservative elements) believe that Muslims and Buddhists are negative influences in America society, while only 15% view them positively.[30] Some elements are not even comfortable with members of old established Christian traditions that interpret Christian doctrine somewhat differently from the way they do. Pat Robertson has said, "You say, 'You're supposed to be nice to the Episcopalians and the Presbyterians and the Methodists and this, that, and the other thing.' Nonsense. I don't have to be nice to the spirit of Anti-Christ."[31] The Christian right is not comfortable with a secular state committed to neutrality and the legal equality of all communities of faith. Its members want to "bring America back to its senses." They want to "take America back" from the Sheilas and the Buddhists and the agnostics and anybody else who does not see things their way.

This is a reactionary movement, a movement which desires to return to the past, to the "good old days." In societies in the past religion tended to pervade all aspects of life. Politics and religion went hand-in-hand, and a common religion was advanced by governmental authority. Religion pervaded public as well as private life and was considered to be essential for social solidarity and the general happiness of the people. This was the set-up in ancient Greece and Rome as well as for medieval and early modern Europe.

A major reason why religion was pushed out of the public sphere was that this arrangement was less than ideal. It was characterized by religious intolerance and bigotry where those whose consciences did not permit them to conform to the official version of truth were persecuted, often to death. Tens of millions were killed in pogroms, religious wars, inquisitions, and other activities in the name of

God's truth. In this context, the secularist doctrines of eighteenth century Europe, which sought to remove religion from the public sphere, made sense. Our own Constitution was one such secularist doctrine. In fact, America was a leader in proposing a new path, one built upon human freedom and a secular state without the authority to limit religious freedom or impose religious tyranny. Here religious pluralism was respected and it was recognized that perhaps religion should be more of a matter of private conscience than one of public concern. In light of this understanding, America, the most religiously pluralistic nation in the world, has escaped many of the more serious problems faced by other nations. As expressed in the aforementioned *U.S. News* article, "Unlike people in other countries, where religious differences have too often turned violent, Americans have co-existed relatively peacefully in one of the most religiously diverse of nations."[32]

Americans have existed relatively peacefully. But there have been exceptions to this peace, as previously noted. And if the Christian right accomplishes its goals, further exceptions will no doubt be in store for us. If the Christian right accomplishes its goals, we will have many more historical examples of religious intolerance and bigotry to cite in the future.

One target of the Christian right in its attempt to achieve its goals and to "take America back" is entertainment television. It is argued that there is not enough "religion" on television and that the religious elements that do find their way onto the screen are often not sufficiently positive. In other words, it is argued that religion is too often belittled and, even more frequently, ignored.

Many people have noted the absence of religion on television, and certainly not all of them have been members of the Christian right. But this element does seem to predominate. One example of Christian conservatives battling to bring religion to television is The Media Research Center of Alexandria, Virginia. The Center has released three reports on religion and television, covering the 1993, 1994, and 1995 seasons (from which I shall quote interchangeably).[33]

The Center basically wants more "religion-friendly" television. But what, according to the Center, constitutes religion-friendly programming? Is it, perhaps, programming that celebrates the rich diversity of America's religious mosaic?

It certainly is not anything that is "New Age-ish." One report cites an episode of "Melrose Place" in which a man asks a woman what she thinks about the soul. She replies, "I don't think of it so much as the soul, as much as energy." She later states, when asked if she believes in heaven, that she used to think of it as a summer camp.[34] This discussion receives a mixed, rather than a positive, score from the Center. One assumes the ideas were not Christian enough.

Also receiving mixed grades were episodes of "Dr. Quinn, Medicine Woman" and "Walker, Texas Ranger" that dealt with both Christianity and Native American religion. It seems that positive marks were not given because the shows "offered morally equivalent treatments" of the two religions.[35]

The Center is not interested in placing any belief system on an equal plane with the Judeo-Christian religions. It is not interested in debate if any opinions involved challenge Judeo-Christian ideas in any way. In one episode of "Earth 2," "[a]fter

Yale prays, Mary, a resident of the Tarian planet, asks, 'Who were you talking to?' Yale responds, 'God . . . [to] ask forgiveness for the harm that [one does].' Mary counters, 'The Tarian way is better: Don't harm.' "[36] This received a mixed mark.

Professing belief in God does not insure a positive or even a mixed mark. "On the May 10 'Love and War' (CBS), a lead character says she believes in God but has a problem with organized religion."[37] This is given a negative grade. It seems that criticism of organized religion is not acceptable.

Doubt is also not acceptable. A teenage girl, on "Life Goes On," felt estranged from God because her boyfriend had contracted AIDS. This received a negative grade.[38] In what could conceivably be taken to be a good religious debate, two characters in "Picket Fences" disagree on how to respond to an incident in which a boy is shot and seriously wounded. One remarks that he was in the temple all night praying for the boy. The other responds, "I don't want to hear any talk about God. . . . No God would let a thirteen-year-old get shot."[39] The Center did not appreciate the doubt expressed by the latter man and gave the incident a mixed mark.

Christians are also not allowed to do bad things. Two toughs working for a mobster threaten a father and son on Fox's "Daddy Dearest." After the threat we learn that they are Catholic, and that one tough is going to a baptism and wants the other to come along.[40] This received a negative rating. One assumes that toughs should be atheists or agnostics, or at least areligious. (What about a tough who espoused a Native American religion? Would that be all right?)

Negative actions are not to be associated with Judeo-Christian religious elements in any way. An episode of "Law & Order" is labeled negative because "a mentally disturbed woman kills her baby daughter because she believes God wanted her to."[41] The Center is not interested in the fact that religiously-oriented delusions are not uncommon among the seriously mentally ill.

Any proclamation or sign of atheism or agnosticism is graded negatively. A man telling a priest that he does not believe in life after death could conceivably be considered a positive discussion of a religious issue. But the Center sees no room for debate on the life-after-death question.[42] That one used to believe in God also does not carry any weight. A character on the ABC movie "Nowhere to Hide" fits into this category, and the show was slapped with a negative score.[43] Another negative mark was received by an episode of "Northern Exposure" in which a man called himself an agnostic. The Center noted that the man was also portrayed as a "credible, positive character."[44] To depict an agnostic is bad enough. To depict him as positive and credible is clearly beyond the pale for the Center.

So what is a religiously friendly portrayal? On "Against the Grain" two couples stop at a restaurant after church. "That is the best sermon I have heard in a long time," says one of the women. The other woman adds, "Oh, I've always loved that passage."[45] On an episode of "Melrose Place" a tearful visit to a confessional leads a young woman to give up prostitution.[46]

The Center's goals are rather transparent. What religion does it want on fiction televison? It says it wants television to reflect religion as it exists in American society. But does it really? Are there no doubters, New Agers, or agnostics in American society? Are they not involved in the religious mix? Are there no bad Catholics? Do all good people go to church or temple? The Center certainly isn't interested in any balanced presentation of religious issues. In the Report on the 1995 season a "mixed" rating by definition "indicates balanced points of view with ultimately no side taken."[47] The Center does not want balance. It wants television to take a side—its side.

What the Center wants is the Judeo-Christian tradition (here Catholics and Jews are included) shown as always great and good, without problems and conflicts related to matters of religious belief and practice. What it wants is promotion for its own point of view, support for the religious orientations it favors. And yes, intolerance and bigotry are involved—against non-believers, non-church-goers, New Agers, doubters, and generally those outside the Judeo-Christian fold. This intolerance and bigotry might not be as blatant as those found elsewhere, but they are certainly there.

Another example of this orientation of the Christian right in regard to television can be seen in Donald Wildmon and his American Family Association. Mere announcement of Norman Lear's sit-com "Sunday Dinner," which dealt with religious and spiritual issues from Lear's liberal point of view, incited Wildmon to threaten to boycott CBS and its advertizers. Wildmon attacked CBS for allowing Lear to "promote his New Age/secular humanist religion."[48] Similarly, Randall Murphree, who keeps an eye on prime time television for Wildmon's AFA, criticized "Northern Exposure" for the particular brand of religion of the characters. He referred to the character Chris Stevens as "a new-age guru" and to the character Shelly Tambo's sense of Catholicism as "extremely immature." Instead, what was needed was depiction of "a strong Christian faith," no doubt one just like Mr. Murphree's.[49]

The *American Family Association Journal*, a monthly magazine for American Family Association members, keeps track of television shows that do and (mostly) do not depict religion and religious characters adequately. Its perspective is similar to that of the Media Research Center, although it does not seem to be as willing to include Judaism in its realm of protected territory. In addition, it calls for boycotts against shows that fall short of its standards and, especially, against corporate advertisers of these shows. One such boycott involved the CBS sitcom "Heartland," which had the temerity to suggest that non-Christians might go to heaven. The following dialogue was reprinted in the *Journal* as part of the rationale for boycotting the show:

Son: Do Jewish people go to heaven, too; I mean, if they're good?

Grandpa: The answer is yes. Everybody that deserves to get into heaven gets in. You just be the best person you can and God takes care of the rest.

Anyone is certainly entitled to disagree with Grandpa's theological conclusion. But is such disagreement really reasonable grounds for a boycott?

Similarly, boycotts were called for ABC's "Moonlighting" for having an angel character make an allusion to reincarnation, and for the ABC sitcom "Have Faith" for showing a priest lose his temper (even though the *Journal* admitted that the priest was a sympathic character who apologizes for yelling).[50] Here nothing but conservative Christian religious beliefs are acceptable, and all Christian religious characters must be shown as good to the core. An episode of NBC's "Law & Order" is singled out for dealing with the case of a priest charged with sexual molestation of boys. It seems that the AFA believes that such real life issues do not belong on television. Its members are urged to boycott Sprint and MCI which advertised on the show.[51] The Association also does not appreciate humor that strays from the straight and narrow. In a call to boycott General Motors for advertising on "The George Wendt Show" (CBS), the *Journal* notes disapprovingly that a character "refers sarcastically to God as 'Big Daddy.' "[52]

A key criticism of these and other groups of the Christian right, and other critics as well, that gets to the heart of the public square issue is the argument that religion is not adequately represented on the tube, that television in this regard does not adequately reflect American society. Because there are so many religious people in the country for whom religion is such an important part of their lives, the argument goes, we should see this reflected on television, an important part of the public square. Michael Medved has made the same point in regard to movies. What if a Martian's only information about the United States "were an interplanetary rent-by-mail service that provided him with video versions of all the latest Hollywood releases?"[53] He would get a terribly skewed view of the country, he argues. Tom Johnson and Sandra Crawford assert that "[t]o millions of Americans, expressions of devotion are as habitual as brushing one's teeth." It follows, they argue, that religious routines and practices should regularly be included on television.[54] I have argued that what they want on television is not a true reflection of American society, but rather of an American society as they would like it to be. This having been said, it is certainly true that we do not see an accurate representation of religion as it exists in American society on fiction television. But should we?

Television is not about mirroring reality. It is about entertaining people (to attract large audiences of potential consumers to sell to advertisers, etc.). This is why we do not see people brushing their teeth or sleeping or reading books or you name the mundane activity on television. People tune in to escape from their mundane existences, not to dwell upon the ordinary. Most aspects of religion are not terribly exciting on a visual medium such as television. People generally turn on the television to be entertained, to get a cheap thrill, to laugh, to get an emotional release or pick-me-up. They do not generally watch for spiritual enlightenment or to see their lives, religious or otherwise, accurately represented. Accordingly "religion friendly" shows that have appeared ("I'll Fly Away," "Against the Grain," "Brooklyn Bridge") have typically failed to attract a sizable audience. According to producer Michael Jacobs, the 1980s sitcom "Amen" only became really successful when it went for a more physical comedy approach and away from life in the church.[55]

Some of these critics suggest that not bringing religion into the public square by way of television, not depicting religion on television in something approaching a representative fashion, actually marginalizes or even denigrates religion in society as a whole. Thomas Skill argues that television might actually "fictionally 'de-legitimize' religious institutions and traditions by symbolically eliminating them from our most pervasive form of popular culture." He adds, "Over time, the consequences of these actions may actually impact the strength and viability of these institutions as a social force in society."[56]

But it could just as easily be argued that religion is as pervasive and strong as it is in American society because it has been relegated to the private sphere to the extent that it has. It has been able to escape the rationalizing trend to which Weber referred. It has not fostered the internecine battles to the extent that it has in other countries where religion is more of a public matter. It has not grown moribund under the stewardship of the state.

And, again, to the extent that it does enter the public sphere, vigilance must be maintained to prevent the possible conflict, bigotry, and intolerance that can result. Television producers repeatedly note that they are afraid that religion made public on television could lead to conflict. Many feel that religious portayals are no-win situations that will only serve to offend one large group or another. As one producer put it, speaking for many of his colleagues, "religion is so hard to deal with. You're always going to offend someone."[57] Religion is a hot button issue that has the potential to alienate millions of viewers, not to mention stir up animosity in society at large.

As Thomas Skill points out, the absence of religion as a major theme in the popular mass media is not a new phenomenon. In a 1949 study Johns-Heine and Gerth reported that there were very few stories with religious themes in mass periodical fiction from 1921 to 1940 (less than 2% of those sampled). In a more recent study of comic strips, Lindsey and Heeren (1992) reported that this type of mass communication had even fewer references to religious themes (.56% of 65,000 comic strips published in the Los Angeles Times from 1979 to 1987).[58] Although conservative media critics S. Robert Lichter, Linda Lichter, and Stanley Rothman argue that the nature of religion on fiction television has changed for the worse over the years, for example, miracles are not celebrated like they used to be, they admit that religion has never played a prominent role on television, especially on prime time fiction shows.[59]

Despite this "neglect" (and maybe, in part, because of it), religion seems to be flourishing in America. High percentages of Americans profess belief in God and attend religious services. There are more churches per capita in the United States than in any other nation in the world. These and related statistics support the conclusion that the United States is the most religious of the Western democracies, and certainly one of the most religious countries on the face of the earth.

These statistics do not soothe the souls of members of the Christian right. What is most important to them is not that people are religious in some way, but that they are religious in a particular way, their way. They might have become increasingly tolerant of Catholics and Jews (though many would dispute this), but non-Judeo-Christian religions and the Sheilas of the world, not to mention non-believers, remain more than suspect. Discomfort with these suspect elements is largely what all this criticism of television is about. It's about bringing everybody on board, on board the ship of the Christian right. And this constitutes the danger of bringing more religion into the public square via television. It could foster more of the religious intolerance and bigotry of which we have already had far too much in our history.

NOTES

1. *U.S. News and World Report*, "Spiritual America," April 4, 1994, p. 49.

2. Stephen Carter, *The Culture of Disbelief* (New York: Doubleday, 1993), p. 8.

3. Derek Davis, "Religious Pluralism and the Quest for Unity in American Life," in *Journal of Church and State* 36 (Spring, 1994), p. 247.

4. Davis, "Religious Pluralism," p. 249.

5. Anson Phelps Stokes and Leo Pfeffer, *Church and State in the United States* (New York: Harper and Row, 1964), p. 7.

6. Davis, "Religious Pluralism," p. 249.

7. Davis, "Religious Pluralism," p. 249.

8. Davis, "Religious Pluralsim," p. 250.

9. Joseph Tussman, *The Supreme Court on Church and State* (New York: Oxford University Press, 1962), pp. 5-6.

10. Davis, "Religious Pluralism," p. 250-251.

11. Robert Handy, *A Christian America: Protestant Hopes and Historical Realities* (New York: Oxford University Press, 1984).

12. Davis, "Religious Pluralism," p. 251.

13. Terry Muck, *Alien Gods on American Turf* (Wheaton, IL: Victor Books, 1990).

14. Davis, "Religious Pluralism," p. 252.

15. Robert Wuthnow, *The Restructuring of American Religion* (Princeton: Princeton University Press, 1988).

16. "Spiritual America," p. 58.

17. Robert Bellah et al. *Habits of the Heart* (Berkeley: University of California Press, 1985), p. 221. Wade Clark Roof, in his book *A Generation of Seekers: The Spiritual Journeys of the Babyboom Generation* (San Francisco: HarperCollins, 1993), also emphasizes the elements of choice, independent thinking, and experimentation.

18. Critics of television, such as Tom Johnson of the Media Research Center and Thomas Skill of the University of Dayton, have noted that television seems more open to this personal, private type of religion than to organized religion. For example, Skill, writing of religion on fictional network television in 1990, notes that "[w]hen it was portrayed . . . it was most often framed as a personal and private activity." Thomas Skill et al., "The Portrayal of Religion and Spirituality on Fictional Network Television," *Review of Religious Research* 35 (March 1994), p. 251.

19. Talcott Parsons, "Christianity and Modern Industrial Society," in Edward A. Tiryakian,

ed., *Sociological Theory, Values, and Socio-Cultural Change* (New York: Free Press, 1963), pp. 33-70.

20. Max Weber, "Science as a Vocation," in Hans Gerth and C. Wright Mills, eds., *From Max Weber: Essays in Sociology* (New York: Oxford University Press, 1981), pp. 129-156. Another alternative, according to Weber, is that religion can become rationalized itself and compete with the secular world views in public.

21. *The New York Times*, January 22, 1996.

22. I first ran into this slogan on a return address label from the John Hagee Ministries.

23. Norman Lear and David Ramage, "Is This a Make-Over or Is It a Cover-Up?" *Los Angeles Times*, May 12, 1995.

24. *Los Angeles Times*, July 6, 1995.

25. As quoted in Davis, "Religious Pluralism," p. 253.

26. Lear and Ramage, "Is This a Make-Over or Is It a Cover-Up?"

27. David Barton, *The Myth of Separation* (Aledo, TX: WallBuilder Press, 1992).

28. Davis, "Religious Pluralism," p. 254.

29. *The New York Times*, January 30, 1996.

30. From a random telephone survey of 1,007 adults in July 1995 by pollster George Barna of Glendale.

31. Lear and Ramage, "Is This a Make-Over or Is It a Cover-Up?"

32. "Spiritual America," pp. 54-56.

33. Thomas Johnson and Sandra Crawford, Media Research Center, "Faith in a Box: Entertainment Television on Religion, 1993" and "Faith in a Box: Entertainment Television on Religion, 1994" and Thomas Johnson, Media Research Center, "Faith in a Box: Entertainment Television on Religion, 1995." The basic conclusion of all three reports is that religion is both seriously underrepresented and ill-served on entertainment television, and that, correspondingly, there should be more religion-friendly programming.

34. Johnson and Crawford, 1993 Report, p. 3.

35. Johnson and Crawford, 1993 Report, p. 8.

36. Johnson, 1995 Report, p. 4.

37. Johnson and Crawford, 1994 Report, p. 5.

38. Johnson and Crawford, 1993 Report, p. 3.

39. Johnson and Crawford, 1994 Report, p. 3.

40. Johnson and Crawford, 1993 Report, p. 5.

41. Johnson, 1995 Report, p. 7.

42. Johnson and Crawford, 1993 Report, p. 3.

43. Johnson and Crawford, 1994 Report, p. 4.

44. Johnson and Crawford, 1994 Report, p. 4.

45. Johnson and Crawford, 1993 Report, p. 3.

46. Johnson and Crawford, 1993 Report, p. 4.

47. Johnson, 1995 Report, p. 2.

48. As quoted in an article by Richard Zoglin, *Time* 137 (June 3, 1991), p. 71.

49. *News and Record* (Greensboro, NC), May 15, 1994.

50. David Cole, "It's Not the Networks That Shy Away From Religion," *Los Angeles Times*, December 8, 1995.

51. *American Family Association Journal*, June, 1995, p. 8.

52. *American Family Association Journal*, May 1995, p. 6.

53. Michael Medved, *Hollywood vs. America* (New York: HarperCollins, 1992), p. 73.

54. Johnson and Crawford, 1993 Report, p. 9.

55. As quoted in *The Gazette* (Montreal), March 6, 1994.

56. Skill et al., "The Portrayal of Religion," p. 265.

57. John Ferre, ed., *Channels of Belief: Religion and American Commercial Television* (Ames: Iowa State University Press, 1990), p. 31.

58. Skill et al., "The Portrayal of Religion," pp. 253-254.

59. "On television religion is relegated mostly to Sunday mornings and televangelists. Clergy are a rarity on prime time, and religious themes are rarer still." "[M]ost religious themes and characters have played in single episodes of series that otherwise features strictly secular fare." S. Robert Lichter, et al., *Prime Time: How TV Portrays American Culture* (Washington, D.C.: Regnery Publishing, 1994), p. 389-390.

12

Reel Arabs and Muslims

Jack G. Shaheen

Fantasy, abandoned by reason, produces impossible monsters.—Goya

As an important artistic and persuasive medium, television does many things on many levels. Functioning as art and entertainment, programs provide information and help shape values. Produced with extraordinary skill, programs present powerful and penetrating messages, serving to educate and helping to condition viewers toward a particular world view. Intentionally or unintentionally, TV's images teach people whom to fear, whom to hate, and whom to love.

To their credit, positive steps recently taken by leaders of America's television networks to shatter myths show that they are sincerely concerned about presenting a view of the world sans stereotypes. As a result of glasnost, writers seldom display the Russian Communist culprit; the mafioso component within the Italian-American community has been reduced to the occasional harmless buffoon. And "greaser," "Mammy/Uncle Mose," and "Chink" images have been relegated to a video Valhalla. Aware that all Americans have special characteristics, producers are embracing a fresh approach to portraying diverse peoples. They now display characters of many different and distinct cultural identities, complete with accents and various shades of color.

In this country, cultural diversity is visible everywhere—on the streets, in shops, and in offices. Such diversity is seen even on prime time television, with one notable exception: America's Muslims and Arabs, their accomplishments and heritage, remain invisible. Although America's eight million plus Arabs and Muslims are an integral part of the American landscape, viewers almost never see accurate portraits; they do not appear as fully human heroes or heroines.

Americans of Arab heritage are not part of the television landscape. Since the beginning, programmers have presented only two Arab-American characters in series. The first was Uncle Tanoose, patriarch of the Williams family, portrayed by Hans Conried in "The Danny Thomas Show" (1953-1971). The second was Corporal Maxwell Klinger, a soldier wearing women's clothing, played by Jamie Farr in "M*A*S*H" (1972-1983).

Given television's recent appreciation of ethnicity, Arab-Americans are both hurt and puzzled as to why programmers never present them in a remotely sympathetic manner, why they remain invisible. Although their customs, traditions, and accomplishments help make America an exceptional nation, their goodness and contributions to society as doctors, grocers, homemakers, lawyers, laborers, and teachers are ignored.

This lack of presence generates wounds. Surely programmers know what happens to young people "when someone with authority" (e.g., the TV programmer) portrays our society and "you are not in it." Such experiences, writes Adrienne Rich, may be disorienting—"a moment of psychic disequilibrium, as if you looked into a mirror and saw nothing."[1]

As of this writing, networks fail to pattern any of their shows after ordinary Arab-Americans. Nor do any programs focus on prominent Americans of Arab descent. For example, characters patterned after noted Arab and Muslim doctors, lawyers, and journalists are not included in programs such as "Chicago Hope," "E.R.," "Murphy Brown," "Law and Order," "News Radio" and "Murder One." No TV movie has depicted the accomplishments of Danny Thomas, Arab-Americans, and others, who established St. Jude's Children's Hospital, in Memphis. To date, TV has not presented characters patterned after men and women like lawyer and consumer advocate Ralph Nader, heart surgeon Dr. Michael DeBakey, UPI's White House correspondent Helen Thomas, radio's Top-40 celebrity Casey Kasem, Secretary of Health and Human Services Donna Shalala, or former government officials such as Chief of Staff John Sununu and Chief of Protocol Selwa Roosevelt.

Ever since the late 1800s America's Arabs and Muslims have contributed much to our country. Like most Americans, they are peaceful, hospitable people providing for the basic needs of their families, and enjoying, respecting, and assisting neighbors, regardless of their race, religion, position, or wealth. Sadly, in lieu of projecting Arab- and Muslim-American notables as an integral part of America's ethnic rainbow, producers opt to denigrate Arabs and Muslims from "over there."

Research reveals that occasionally a few stock villains appear: Latino drug dealers, sadistic Nazis, corrupt politicians, and cutthroat business persons. Yet, since 1974, when this writer initially began documenting the Arab and Muslim image on entertainment shows, the predominant rogues have been Arab and Muslim ones, including boisterous billionaires, bombastic bombers, backward Bedouins, belly dancers, boring harem maidens, and submissive domestics.

For more than two decades, odious portraits and themes have presented both the Arab and the Muslim as a bogeyperson, the dangerously threatening Cultural Other. Image makers ignore their hospitality, rich culture, and history, failing to understand many basic facts about Arabs and Muslims. For example, they do not realize that Islam is a faith embraced by 1.2 billion people, including 250 million

Arabs in 21 nations. Also, Islam is the fastest growing of the universal religions. It is estimated that by the year 2000 Muslims will constitute 27% of the world's population. Approximately 15 million Christians reside in Arab countries, and the majority of America's 3 million Arab-Americans are Christians. Five to eight million Muslims live in the United States. "There are more than 200,000 Muslim businesses, 1,200 mosques, 165 Islamic schools, 425 Muslim associations and 85 Islamic publications."[2]

Damaging portraits are not harmless cliches. There is a dangerous cumulative effect in repeated images, especially those left unchallenged. And TV shows, like books, last forever. Once the Arab and Muslim surfaces as the quintessential Other, ugly portraits assume a life of their own, communicating for generations a hate-the-Arab/Muslim message.

My research work demonstrates that Arabs and Muslims are consistently portrayed in a stereotypical manner. Presented here is a selective overview and analysis taken from hundreds of TV programs, including comedies, soap operas, children's cartoons, dramas, and movies-of-the-week.

To illustrate that entertainment television is not the only medium offering Arab and Muslim caricatures, I will show how the image found on entertainment TV prowls other media, referring to TV newscasts and news magazines, documentaries, and motion pictures. As with the TV image, more than 800 feature films and scores of documentaries show the Arab-Muslim sans a humane face.

TELEVISION MOVIES

Englishman John Buchan declared in his popular 1916 novel *Greenmantle*, "Islam is a fighting creed, and the mullah still stands in the pulpit with the Koran in one hand and a drawn sword in the other."[3] Approximately seventy years later, viewers see clones of Buchan's mullah in motion-pictures-made-for-television. The TV films present especially injurious portraits, narrowing our vision and blurring reality.

The TV movie genre gives the impression that all Arab Muslims are terrorists. The following five TV-movies advancing this stereotypical image appeared during the mid- and late 1980s. Yet they all—"Hostage Flight" (NBC, 1985), "Sword of Gideon" (HBO, 1986), "Under Siege" (NBC, 1986), "The Taking of Flight 847" (NBC, 1980), and "Terrorist on Trial: The United States vs. Salim Ajami" (CBS, 1988)—regularly emerge as reruns on cable and network systems.

Screen Arabs and Muslims resemble yesterday's images of Hitler's SS and Attila's hordes. Throughout each of these TV movies, the Arab Muslim lurks in the shadows. Armed with an AK-47, dagger, or bomb, he proceeds to rape, beat, and murder innocent Americans. In "Hostage Flight," a passenger aboard an airplane hijacked by "terrorists" says: "These (Arab) bastards shot those people in cold blood. They think it's open season on Americans."

In "Under Siege," Muslim fanatics invade the United States, blowing up 200-

plus soldiers. A White House official says: "They're Shi'ite terrorists. . . . [W]e all knew they would hit us at home." Several scenes show the "terrorists" killing innocents on street corners, in restaurants, and at airports. Finally, with the assistance of Arab-Americans in Dearborn, Michigan, they proceed to blow up the White House. An FBI official orders his men to check out "every Middle East community" (in the United States). He adds, "There's a large Shi'ite community in the Detroit area." Superimposed on the screen we see: "Dearborn, Michigan." This is followed by shots of stores with Arab names and signs with Arabic lettering. By projecting, in this fictional TV movie, the Detroit/Dearborn community as a haven for Muslim and Arab terrorists, the producers employ racism.

The producers of this fiction film should have employed a fictitious city, or a place where few or no American Muslims and Arabs reside. When they state that Arab and Muslim terrorists are operating out of the Detroit/Dearborn area, the largest Arab-American and Muslim community in the United States, the producers not only cross the line between fictional images and real portraits, they endanger innocents. Although in reality Detroit/Dearborn is home to more than a half-million peace-loving and law-abiding Arab-Americans, some viewers could easily believe the opposite.

Even the dialogue is racist. The U.S. Secretary tells Iran's Ambassador: "People in your country are barbarians." The FBI director jumps in, telling his colleague: "Those people [Arabs] are different from us. It's a whole different ball game. I mean the East and the Middle East. These people have their own mentality. They have their own notion of what's right and what's wrong, what's worth living for and dying for. But we insist on dealing with them as if they're the same as us. We'd better wake up."

Finally, the two writers of "Siege," one of whom is Pulitzer Prize–winner Bob Woodward, mistakenly informs viewers that Iranians are Arabs. These writers do not know that Iranians are Persians, a people speaking Farsi, and not Arabs speaking Arabic.

"Terrorist on Trial" focuses on Ajami, a Palestinian Arab who is a heartless fanatic opposed to peace. He is captured in the Middle East and brought to trial in the United States. Ajami has no regrets about ordering the deaths of American women and children and admits that he would even use nuclear weapons. "We will strike at them in their home country as well as overseas. Long live Palestine!"

One protagonist explains that Palestinian Arabs, not just Ajami, "prefer to walk up to unarmed people and shoot them." A noted journalist says Arabs and Muslims are more violent, more primitive than others. "They appeal to our sympathy by calling themselves 'guerrillas or freedom fighters.' They're not." And Ajami's defense attorney requests that the jury view the Palestinian as "someone who might as well have been from another planet." Finally, ignoring the contributions of Ralph Nader and other prominent Arab-American lawyers who contribute much to our country, the writers have a Justice Department official say: "A fact is a fact. There are no qualified American-Arab attorneys to defend Ajami."

What is so disquieting about these TV movies is that they effectively show all

Arabs, Muslims, and Arab-Americans as being at war with the United States. Nicholas Kadi, an Arab-American performer who earns a living playing mostly Arab terrorists, is uneasy about his craft. Relegated to playing an Arab terrorist in the short-lived series "The Last Precinct," Kadi says he "did little talking and a lot of threatening—threatening looks, threatening gestures, threatening actions. Every time we [he and others playing Arab heavies] said 'America,' we'd spit." Explains Kadi, "There are other kinds of Arabs in the world besides terrorists. I'd like to think that some day there will be an Arab role out there for me that would be an honest portrayal."[4] Yet, a decade after Kadi's plea for balance, the situation on television remains static. (More on this actor later in the essay.)

As with all groups, a small minority within the minority are heavies. Although terrorism is a legitimate screen theme, to paint all members of any group of people, in this case Arabs, with the same negative brush is morally and ethically wrong. Over the years television's monochromatic images have wrongly perpetuated the myth that all Arabs possess a violent gene, that they are not human like us and deserve to die. The terrorism theme has only been exploited, never seriously addressed. No TV movie remotely approaches the complexity of the terrorist bombings in "The Battle of Algiers" or the kidnapping-execution in "State of Siege." In these classic works of film art, the characters are portrayed with subtlety and precision.

Producers permit viewers to see Arabs and Muslims only as perpetrators of violence, never as victims. TV movies and specials never show images of Palestinians struggling to live under Israeli occupation. The camera does not reveal Palestinian homes being destroyed or families coping with poor living conditions in refugee camps. Nor do viewers see Palestinian arms being broken, or demonstrators being shot dead. Nor are apolitical images projected. Viewers do not see the Arab mother singing to her child. They do not see a doctor tending the ill, a teacher giving a lesson in biology, a programmer working with computer software. An Arab man never embraces his wife. Families do not picnic or go to mosque or church. To paraphrase journalist Edward R. Murrow, what we do not see is as important as, if not more important than, what we do see.

What do writers intend to accomplish by singling out one group of people for humiliation? Appropriately, the TV terrorist movies of the 1980s did not vilify the Campolongos, Goldsteins, Gonzaleses, O'Reillys, or Yammamotos. To do so would invite charges of racism, engendering an onslaught of critical media coverage and protests.

Although network officials may boast that they do not unfavorably stereotype individuals of any ethnic origin, when it comes to Arabs, Muslims, and Americans of Arab heritage that is exactly what the industry has done. Consider NBC-TV's Broadcast Standards manual which states, "Television programs should reflect a wide range of roles for all people . . . and should endeavor to depict men, women, and children in a positive manner, keeping in mind the importance of dignity in every human being."[5] To date, network practice has yet to follow network policy. The sins of omission and commission continue.

DRAMAS

Talented Arab-American performers such as Nicholas Kadi are obliged to demean their heritage. Although Kadi is a highly competent character actor, producers cast him primarily as a kuffiyeh-clad heavy. As Kadi explained on CBS-TV's "48 Hours,"[6] if he wants to work, he is obliged to portray evil Arabs in films such as "Navy Seals" (1990), and in TV shows such as NBC's "JAG" episode "Scimitar."[7]

In "Scimitar" the Iraqi-born Kadi impersonates a Saddam-like colonel holding an innocent U.S. Marine hostage. The lusting Kadi tries forcing himself on Meg, an attractive blond U.S. naval officer. And why not? One TV myth maintains that Arabs consider "date rape" to be "an acceptable social practice." The camera shows drooling Kadi using a "Damascus scimitar" to slowly remove Meg's uniform.

"JAG" producers and others demean today's Arab as television and film makers once demonized Indians. Clad in strange garb, both Arabs and Indians speak muddled dialogue and lust after blonde heroines. Just as screen protagonists called Indians "savages," they today label Arabs "terrorists." The following sequence denotes the stereotypical commonalities. "Scimitar" concludes with Kadi being killed. Watching an Iraqi helicopter which had been pursuing them go down in flames, the American protagonists cheer. "Yahoo. It's just like 'Stagecoach,' " says a U.S. Marine, "with John Wayne." The puzzled Meg asks: "John Wayne was killed by Iraqis?" The reply, "Indians!"

Even Hulk Hogan clobbers Arabs. In a "Thunder in Paradise" two-part program set in the mythical kingdom of Mogador, Arabs imprison Hogan and friends.[8] Meanwhile, gobs of clad-in-black rogues try to force Kelly, the heroine, to marry a fierce-looking Arab giant. Our heroes escape by duping the dense guard, convincing him that his food is camel dung. Hogan and his party proceed to beat up the Arab giant and rescue Kelly. As the new champion, Hogan is given scores of mute ladies-in-waiting. The only catch is that Hogan must have an operation making him a eunuch. Opting to depart, our hero punches out the King's son, "a royal wimp," and he and his pals escape. In the process, they blow scores of Arab heavies to smithereens.

COMEDIES

Arabs are degraded on two "Married . . . With Children" segments. In one, a couple clad in Arab garb inquire about a car for sale. One carries a homemade bomb in his hand; he threatens the vehicle's owner.[9] In the other, Al Bundy questions Peg, his wife, about her reckless spending. Asks Al: "How about the kids, Peg? Did they really go to your mother's house or do they belong to the Arabs now?" The audience howls![10]

A "Small Wonder" segment features Akeem, a 13-year-old rich Arab sheikh complete with harem who is tagged a "camel jockey."[11] Akeem is out to acquire Vickie Lawson as his bride. He gives her a diamond ring the size of "a large grape."

"Camel breath!" Vickie shouts at Moustafa, Akeem's rotund guardian. No one counters the slur. Mr. and Mrs. Lawson associate with Akeem only because Mr. Lawson wants to secure a "multimillion (dollar) contract." In exchange for Vickie, Akeem offers to give the mute Araba, one of his maidens, to Jamie, Vickie's brother. Akeem wants Vickie for two reasons. One, she is an American; the other, Vickie seems "obedient." He tells her, "You must do as I say and fluff my pillows." Barks Vickie, "You can fluff your own pillows, turkey." She adds, "You clap your hands one more time at me, Buster, and I'll fluff your mouth." The Arab-mocking dialogue and scenes continue until the show's closing minutes. During the final scenes, Arabs and Americans separate. Akeem does not wed Vickie and Jamie returns Araba. But the Lawsons do get the contract.

SOAP OPERAS

This writer never watched the soaps until a few years ago, when, as I was conducting a workshop for secondary school teachers in Madison, Wisconsin, I asked whether anyone was aware of stereotypical Arabs and Muslims. "I think so," said one teacher. "There are some strange types on 'Santa Barbara.' "[12]

Since then, I have studied Arab images in "Santa Barbara," "Loving," and "The Bold and the Beautiful." As some of the settings and Arab characters in "Santa Barbara" are similar to those in "Loving" and "Beautiful," I will limit my comments to this soap. Daily, for several weeks during the summer of 1990, I taped and studied "Santa Barbara" when two shady sheikhs were at war with each other. The story shows both potentates holding Americans hostage and fighting each other. The Sheikh of Kabir is intent on invading the neighboring "two-bit country" called Khareef. Kabir's ruler executed the Pasha of Khareef's "mother and father and two sisters" right before his "very eyes."

The pasha has "sacred ways," including "a harem." None of his wives please him; he lusts for Eden, the American blond. And he intends to execute a wife because she dared run off. Not to do so would mean "losing face." He boasts that "to take advice from a woman is equal to a bubble floating on air." In the end, the American hostages are released, Kabir's evil ruler is toppled, and the Pasha promises Eden he will eliminate his "prejudice" against women.

Soaps such as NBC-TV's "Santa Barbara," CBS-TV's "The Bold and the Beautiful," and ABC-TV's "Loving" teach viewers that Arabs live in tents, hold Americans hostage, have harems, dislike and/or torment their own women, and act in a humane manner only when accompanied by an American woman.

CHILDREN'S CARTOONS

Ever since the 1926 cartoon "Felix the Cat Shatters the Sheik," America's cartoon champions have denigrated Arabs and Muslims. Beginning in 1975, I have monitored and studied TV cartoon shows. Though incomplete, my research reveals that 60-plus animated cartoons feature heroes—Inspector Gadget, Popeye, Bugs Bunny, the Pink Panther, Porky Pig, and others—trouncing and ridiculing Arabs. Animators paint Arabs as swine, rats, dogs, magpies, vultures, and monkeys. Posing as Arab women, animated woodpeckers and rabbits don harem outfits and feign belly dancing. Selected to be a lecherous sheikh's "75th bride," even Popeye dons harem garb. As for Olive Oyl, she would "rather starve to death than marry" the Arab.

Writers tag cartoon Arabs "Sheikh Ha-Mean-Ie," "Ali Boo-Boo," "The Phoney Pharaoh," "Hajji Baba and the Forty Thieves," "Fast Abdul, the Sneakiest Thief in Town," "A Wolf in Sheikh's Clothing," "Ali Baba, the Mad Dog of the Desert," "Ali Ben Schemer," "Hassan the Assassin," "The Desert Rat," and "Desert Rat Hordes." These names and images that producers attribute to Arabs are not benign. Some adults may be able to separate fact from the stereotype. But for most children the animated world of cartoons is simple; it consists of good people versus bad people, for example, Batman versus Arabs.

The animated Bedouin and sheikh caricatures are variations of yesterday's hateful portraits of the stereotypical dense African American and savage Native American. Resembling the brutal "Buck" and the fierce "Injun," the unkempt Bedouin brigand appears as an uncivilized character, a cultural Other. By cultural Other, I mean someone who appears, speaks, and acts differently from the typical white Westerner, someone of a different race and/or national origin. Wearing "different" garb, the cultural Other possesses an "unusual" set of characteristics and looks unlike the typical Westerner. Like the painted face of the animated "Chief Ugh-A-Mug," the Bedouin in bed sheets speaks broken English. Representing evil, both the Bedouin and the Indian attack innocents in forts. Symbolizing the forces of goodness, characters such as Porky Pig and Bugs Bunny repel the charging villains.

When viewing such scenarios, especially those in which sheikhs resemble bucktoothed "Japs"or Shylocks with burnooses, some families are reminded of identical messages from which Jewish mothers in the Europe of the 1930s, and Japanese mothers in the United States of the 1940s, tried so hard to shield their children.

When focusing on Islam, especially offensive are "Inspector Gadget" and "Heathcliff," cartoons showing animated Muslims not glorifying God but idolizing Westerners. In "Heathcliff," Egyptians believe the cat to be their ancient ruler and continually prostrate themselves. When Gadget discovers an ancient relic, Muslims repeatedly bow, mumbling "the chosen one, the chosen one."

There is insufficient understanding and concern within the American entertainment community of the damaging nature of these cartoon images. For example, in his October 1995 Variety story, writer Peter Warg is very critical of Kuwait's Muslims because, instead of purchasing and telecasting U.S. cartoons that demean Arabs, they want to begin producing and projecting Islamic animated cartoons, featuring Arab champions.[13] Kuwaiti Muslims are ridiculed for expressing legitimate concerns about the effect American cartoon images have on Arab children. Also, Variety adds insult to injury by displaying a color illustration resembling

TV's cartoon Muslims along with the essay. The picture shows several militant desert Arabs, sabers and rifles raised, about to mow down Tom and Jerry, who are tied to the stake. What prompted *Variety* to brandish such a color sketch, mocking Arabs? Consider this: Had some Asians or Africans expressed similar concerns about the impact of U.S. cartoons being telecast in their nations, would *Variety* have published a stereotypical sketch, mocking them?

Missing from Warg's story is the fact that Americans are never disgraced in Arab children's cartoons. Moreover, 80% of the programs telecast by Kuwait TV's English Channel are American imports. Although U.S. distributors earn millions from these syndicated TV shows, profits flow in only one direction: from Arab to U.S. pockets. Our networks never import and telecast Arab cartoons or other TV entertainment programs.

FEATURE FILMS TELECAST ON TV

The focus of this essay concerns television, but it is significant to understand that soon after Hollywood's features depart from movie theaters they are transmitted onto TV screens. Beginning in 1986, I began tracking features that were being telecast on cable and network channels in St. Louis, Missouri. The research reveals that each week fifteen to twenty movies ridicule and/or denigrate Arabs. TV viewers witness scores of motion pictures such as "Navy Seals" (1990), "Killing Streets" (1991), "The Human Shield" (1992), "The Son of the Pink Panther" (1993), "Bloodfist V:Human Target" (1994), and "True Lies" (1994), a film showing Arab-Muslim villains igniting an atomic bomb in the Florida Keys. These movies and others feature U.S. agents and military personnel, as well as Inspector Clouseau's son, massacring pesky Arabs.

Especially disturbing is the fact that unsightly Arabs are inserted into movies shown on television which have nothing to do with Arabs or the Middle East, films such as "Network" (1976), "Reds" (1981), "Cloak and Dagger" (1984), "Power" (1986), "Puppet Master II" (1990), "Patriot Games" (1992), and others. Surprising Arab caricatures are fastened into the viewer's consciousness at unwarranted times, like insistent unforeseen phantoms. In these movies the inserted Arab characters generally have little to do with the story line. Yet, to date, Hollywood studios have released more than two hundred of them, many of which are telecast. The first of these movies was Universal's "The Rage of Paris" (1921). Here, the Western heroine's husband "is killed in a sandstorm by an Arab." Currently, Libyans are a target. In "Back to the Future" (1985), "Broadcast News" (1987), and "Patriot Games" (1992), Libyan "bastards" shelter Irish villains, bomb U.S. military installations in Italy, and shoot "our" heroic scientist in a mall parking lot!

Columbia's "The American President" (1995) is an agreeable romantic comedy about a widowed president falling for a lovely environmental lobbyist. Yet, Libyans appear as culprits who bomb a U.S. weapons system. (It should be noted that writer Aaron Sorkin does soften the anti-Libyan dialogue by extending sympathy for the Arab janitor and other innocents about to be bombed.)

History illustrates that although the industry is trying to curb biases, even family feel-good films denigrate Arabs. In 1995, Touchstone Pictures, a subsidiary of the Walt Disney Company, released yet another screen rendition of Edward Streeter's 1948 book *Father of the Bride*. The Disney film, "Father of the Bride, Part II," which is the fourth film based on Streeter's work, was listed for months among the top ten weekly money-makers. According to *Entertainment Weekly*, the sixteenth-ranked "Bride II" has become a booming money-maker, grossing more than $80 million for the studio.[14]

Arab-Americans and Muslims, however, do not share Disney's enthusiasm. They are troubled by the unwarranted appearance of disagreeable Arab-Americans in "Bride II." Beginning with the original 1950 Spencer Tracy–Elizabeth Taylor film, all "Father of the Bride" movies have focused on marriage and love. "Bride II" is a sequel to the 1991 Steve Martin remake. Muslims and Americans of Arab heritage do not appear in any of the earlier versions. So, what prompted Disney to inject stereotypes in its 1995 "Bride II"?

Consider the plot. Martin and Diane Keaton appear as the happily married Bankses; they have everything, including a wonderful "Brady Bunch" home. When George convinces Nina to sell it, an Arab-American couple surfaces: the crass Habibs. The film's ferocious Doberman pinschers behave better than this disagreeable duo. The rich, unfeeling, and unkempt Habib (Eugene Levy) smokes, needs a shave, and talks with a weighty accent. When his wife attempts to speak, Habib barks, in what is supposedly Arabic, mumbo-jumbo at her. Cowering like a scolded puppy, Mrs. Habib shrinks and becomes mute, perpetuating Hollywood's stale image of the Arab woman as a mute, submissive nonentity. Blurts Habib to George: "When can you move? You sell, we pay top dollar!" Habib purchases the house, insisting that the Bankses "be out in ten days." George and daughter Annie (Kimberly Williams) rush back to their Maple Drive residence to rekindle memories. Music underscores sentiments as father and daughter recall the times when they carved their initials on a tree and played basketball.

Abruptly, the music changes. Habib enters the frame, commanding, "You got a key, George? The key!" As George and Annie fondly view the house, Habib tosses his cigarette and crushes it on the immaculate walkway. The message is clear: there goes the neighborhood.

Not if George can help it! When Habib steers a huge yellow wrecking ball toward the house, George flings himself in front of the driving ball. Pleads George, "I built this fence; I planted this grass. Don't bulldoze my memories, man! I'm begging you." Habib proceeds to rip-off George. Though Habib owned the house for just one day, he will return it, provided there is profit. Only after extorting $100,000 from George does Habib halt the wrecking ball.

As *Entertainment Weekly's* Ken Tucker writes, "The caricature of a cold, rich . . . [Habib] amounts to a glaring ethnic slur."[15]

Regrettably, no screen professionals affiliated with "Bride II" denounced the stereotypes. Nor did protests emanate from members of the Screen Writers', Actors', and Directors' Guilds of America.

"Bride II" could easily have projected the Habibs as a regular Arab or Muslim-American couple with likable children. Featuring the Habibs as helpful acquaintances, whom the Bankses befriend, would be a more accurate image. Unlike Disney's stereotypical Habibs, most of America's Arabs and Muslims (as well as those outside of the United States) are, like most people, caring human beings and responsible citizens.

Sadly, the tainted writing of "Bride II" ignores this reality, bringing to mind other narrow-minded authors, such as those responsible for the "Club Paradise" (1986) screenplay. This script, too, includes an Arab cur. Like the Habib of "Bride II," the mute white-robed sheikh of "Paradise" cares only about money. Not concerned about the environment or people, the sheikh seeks to destroy a Caribbean paradise, threatening to build factories, high-rise condos, and even a hideous Arabian palace.

Similarly, in "Earthbound" (1980), the scenario focuses on adorable Americans, much like the Bankses. Here, rural Americans befriend an outer space family. Although the film has nothing to do with the Middle East, the producers inject a mute burnoosed sheikh threatening to ruin "our" environment. This Arab wants to buy a picturesque hotel and replace it with "a twenty-story monstrosity." The American owner laments that the sheikh is trying to "sell my hotel right from under me" so he "can build condominiums." But he insists that "not on this land" will such construction occur. All ends well, as the plot to snatch the hotel is foiled.

There are numerous similarities in the three previously discussed movies. Armed with gobs of money, those Arabs from over there come here to destroy our cherished landscapes. Viewers see the scheming sheikh of "Earthbound" trying to ravage the environment by erecting American condos. And the covetous sheikh in "Paradise" attempts to demolish the Caribbean landscape. Finally, in "Bride II" the conniving Arab-American not only wrings $100,000 from Steve Martin but he also nearly demolishes Martin's quaint Los Angeles home.

Disney, responsible for "Bride II," is the same studio that demeaned Arabs in "Aladdin" (1992), the second most successful animated picture ever. Although sensitivity meetings between Arab-Americans and Disney executives following the release of "Aladdin" led Disney to promise not to demean Arabs in the future, the studio went ahead a short time later and trounced Arabs again by projecting several hook-nosed, buck-toothed Arab "desert skunks" in its home video release "The Return of Jafar" (1994). Disturbingly, in lieu of honoring their commitment to eradicate the stereotype, Disney continued to vilify Arabs and Muslims.

In July 1993, the studio tossed a scrawny bone to concerned Arab-American watchdogs, deleting two offensive lines from "Aladdin's" opening lyrics from home videos. That was it! The line "It's barbaric, but hey, it's home," remains. As a July 14, 1993, *New York Times* editorial, "It's Racist, but Hey, It's Disney," points out, "That's progress, but still unacceptable. To characterize an entire region with this sort of tongue-in-cheek bigotry, especially in a movie aimed at children, borders on barbaric."

Those acquiring the "Aladdin" video still hear the region being tagged a "barbaric" place, still see all the unsightly stereotypes. Disney could easily have edited the video's opening scenes and presented viewers with a distinguished story teller such as Damascus' Abu Shadi, a poet and expert teller of tales. Instead, Disney's "Aladdin" presents viewers with a shifty, disreputable story teller. Also, through-out, viewers still see dastardly scimitar-wielding villains trying to cut off the hands of needy maidens, ugly shop keepers, and guards, and a wicked vizier getting his kicks by "slicing a few throats." For generations such scenes will teach children that Aladdin's home is, indeed, "barbaric."

EFFECT

Image makers engaged in defaming peoples should heed Bill Watterson's in-sights. In his *Calvin and Hobbes Tenth Anniversary Book,* Watterson writes that, like TV shows, "Comic strips have historically been full of ugly stereotypes, the hallmark of writers too lazy to honestly observe the world." Declares Watterson, "The cartoonist who resorts to stereotypes reveals his [or her] bigotry."[16]

Should not writers be held accountable for their caricatures? How much longer will professionals be able to present repulsive images of Arabs and Muslims and get away with it? Haven't they learned that damaging words and pictures have a telling effect, that images serve as teaching devices, instructing peoples on whom to despise?

Not so long ago, television images advised viewers that the Asian was "sneaky"; the black, "Sambo"; the Italian, "a Mafia member"; the Irishman, "a drunk"; and the Hispanic, "greasy." Fortunately, such offensive labeling is no longer tolerated. So, why continue painting Arabs as cultural Others? Explains Sam Keen, author of *Faces of the Enemy* (1986), "You can hit an Arab free; they're free enemies, free villains—where you couldn't do it to a Jew or you can't do it to a black any-more."[17]

The time is long overdue for image makers to begin eradicating portraits that cause harm. Television's caricatures afflict innocents. Cliches do not exist in a vacuum. They engender among America's Arabs and Muslims feelings of insecu-rity, vulnerability, and alienation, and can even lead to denial of one's heritage.

As scholar Alfred C. Richard, Jr. points out, media systems provide "an excel-lent reflection of a nation's collective mentality, [and] its national consciousness."[18]

Make no mistake. The "bad Arab-Muslim" stereotype is firmly embedded in America's "collective mentality." For example, consider the aftermath of the April 19, 1995, bombing of the Alfred Murrah Federal Building in Oklahoma City. The two American-born men indicted for the crime, Timothy J. McVeigh and Terry L. Nichols, are not Muslims; nor do they possess Arab roots. They are considered to have been driven by political beliefs. Appropriately, journalists have not discussed the suspects' faith or heritage.

Nevertheless, immediately after the Oklahoma City bombing reporters initially and wrongly speculated for sixty-plus hours that the tragedy was brought about by "Middle Eastern" terrorism, by people who looked "Middle Eastern." As documented by the Council on American-Islamic Relations (CAIR) special report, *A Rush to Judgment*, such speculation resulted in more than two hundred hate crimes being committed against Muslims and Arab-Americans. Eight mosques were vandalized and burned to the ground; innocents were beaten, harassed, and humiliated at work. Fearing violence, some closed their businesses. Finally, hours after the initial reports pointing fingers at Middle Easterners, an angry mob began stoning a pregnant American Muslim woman's Oklahoma City home. During the unwarranted attack, she lost her child.[19]

Many Americans who believed those journalists who incorrectly reported that the bomber was someone who looked "Middle Eastern" did so because of preconditioning. For decades, TV entertainment programs, as well as TV news programs and specials, have demonized Arabs and Muslims, tagging them as "terrorists," "radicals," "militants," and "fanatics."

This writer, like most Americans, regards a news program as an honest attempt at offering an unbiased examination of important issues that have been explored fairly, resulting in credible information to viewers. But even television news programs contain diatribes against Muslims. Almost no effort is made to ensure accuracy, depth, fairness, or objectivity. Some journalists, like some illusion inventors, perpetuate the myth that Muslims hate "civilized" peoples, notably Americans and Israelis.

Several weeks prior to the November 1994 telecast of his Public Broadcasting System news special, "Jihad in America!,"[20] journalist Steven Emerson appeared on CBS-TV's "Eye On America" slandering Muslims.[21] He asserted that money is being raised by America's Arabs and Muslims for a "holy war" here and in the Middle East. On November 13, 1994, CBS-TV's "60 Minutes" displayed Emerson preaching a similar gospel. Finally, on November 27, Emerson's "Jihad!" featured the journalist telling Americans that it seemed "inevitable" that they would be attacked by "Muslim radicals."

The monolithic Muslim portraits of "Jihad!" have been seen on other documentaries presented on PBS, such as "The Islamic Bomb"[22] and "The Sword of Islam."[23] Documentary images of Muslims as fanatics are similar to portraits in entertainment shows. "Sword" was telecast on PBS on January 10, 1994, only two days after CBS-TV presented its Muslim-as-bogeyman TV-movie "Terrorist on Trial."[24]

Continuously pounded into psyches, abhorrent words and images in news shows help ignite the fires of bigotry. What journalists say and project can have grave consequences. As a result of poisonous images some peace-loving Muslims who love and genuinely respect the United States may be victimized by vicious slurs and/or hate crimes. For example, on March 23, 1996, employees of a Denver radio station burst into a Denver mosque and began harassing worshipers. The station broadcast the incident live. One DJ played the national anthem on a trumpet; another donned a mock turban and a Mahmoud Abdul-Rauf T-shirt. The assaults launched against Muslims by Denver's DJs affirms that there is a commanding link between reel images and reality.[25]

Producers fail to take into account that in all groups there are some rotten apples, a tiny minority of destructive, violent people.

Prejudice thrives on defaming stereotypes; as a *New York Times* editorial pointed out in July 1993, "Most Americans now know better than to use nasty generalizations about ethnic or religious groups." Yet, "one form of ethnic bigotry retains an aura of respectability in the United States," that is, prejudice against Arabs (and Muslims).[26]

Ultimately, it is the continual stain of indelible portraits that hurts most. The images are permanent. They may never be erased. The accumulated resonance of these pictures in the minds of America's Arabs and Muslims takes its toll over time. This may explain why many firmly believe that all TV producers not only hate them but despise their religion and heritage. During the May 1995 annual American-Arab Anti-Discrimination Committee (ADC) conference in Washington, D.C., an Arab-American girl approached the guest speaker, ABC-TV's Sam Donaldson, and asked the journalist, "Why do you hate us?"

In 1980, the editors of *The New Republic* wrote: "Arabs [and Muslims] have been the victims of ugly racial stereotypes in recent years . . . [and] the widespread casual violation of such standards [against this] threatens all potential victims of racial slurs. It ought to stop."[27]

It hasn't stopped. The Arab remains a favorite target.

On "The Jon Stewart Show," "Talk Show Jon" displays U.S. soldier puppets killing white-robed Arab puppets. Waving the American flag, one solder boasts: "I killed many of them." Brags another: "I decapitated quite a few of them myself." Immediately, Stewart's live audience applauded![28]

In "Twisted Puppet Theater," Ali, the Arab puppet sporting a black beard and turban, shouts: "There is only one God and Mohammed is his prophet." Then Ali shoots Kukla, the good clown puppet, dead![29]

In an episode of the "X-Files," a mute Muslim agent and "Mohammad," his associate, appear and are immediately killed after they attack Lauren, the episode's heroine. Viewers are told that the two dead Muslims belonged to an "exiled extremist group operating in the United States," that they are responsible for "a July bombing of a navy transport van," and that they "killed a couple of sailors in Florida."[30]

In a July, 1994, "TimeTrax" segment entitled "The Gravity of It All," inept Arab kidnappers/assassins are out to steal advanced U.S. tactical weapons. Operating in Malibu, they are punched out and killed by the American protagonist.[31]

DISPELLING A STEREOTYPE

Negative stereotypes take a long time to wither away. For example, consider the criticism leveled at Laila Lalami, a doctoral degree candidate in linguistics at the University of Southern California. Ms. Lalami wrote an Op-Ed essay for the *Los Angeles Times* critical of "Bride II."[32] One week later the *Times* published an essay by actor Terrence Beasor, who dismissed the possibility that Arab caricatures might have negative effects on somebody. Beasor advised Ms. Lalami to "cheer up." He wrote that stereotypes are a "time-honored tradition" and "not based on racial or gender bias."[33]

Countered Casey Kasem in a letter to the *Times*, "Historically, that's [i.e., that "time honored tradition" is] exactly what such slurs are based on. It's the thoughtless dismissal of the consequences that allows the practice of slurring to continue doing its harm." Kasem concluded with this sentence, which the *Times* did not publish: "Perhaps if everyone named Beasor had been the target of negative stereotyping for the past seventy-five years, the writer might have had some small idea what it's like to grow up on the receiving end of dehumanizing prejudice."[34]

In time, prejudices may evaporate, provided one keeps in mind the basic law of physics which states, "Nothing percolates unless you apply heat." One way to provide sufficient heat would be if the prestigious Disney Channel and Disney Studios led the way in debunking harmful myths. By inserting ordinary Arabs and Muslims in their programs, Disney could lead the way, encouraging other image makers not to "do it" to an Arab or Muslim "anymore."

To their credit, Disney's weekly TV series, "Aladdin," offers, in lieu of stereotypes, mostly balanced and heroic Arab portraits. And during 1995, Disney executives permitted Arab-Americans to peruse the screenplay of its upcoming home video "Aladdin and the King of Thieves." One reader of "Thieves" was Media Coalition President Don Bustany, who told this writer the teleplay was devoid of stereotypes.

Yet, Disney has not employed any Arab-Americans or Muslims to do voiceovers for "Thieves." Nor are Arab-Americans on the scene, regularly consulting with writers and animators. Their presence certainly would sensitize image makers and surely lead to more faithful and diverse portraits of the peoples and their cultures on television entertainment programs.

For example, to insure that hurtful images would not appear in its successful "Pocahontas," Disney went to great lengths to win the endorsement of Native Americans. Not wishing to repeat its experiences with "Aladdin," the studio was resolved to avoid caricatures. This time it sought out and hired Native American leaders to work on the film and to act as consultants.

The studio cast American Indian performers such as actress Irene Bedard to be the voice of Pocahontas, and Russell Means as the voice of Pocahontas's father, Chief Powhatan. Means, a well-known American Indian, praised the Disney film: "Looking at it as an American Indian, I cannot find anything wrong with this movie. I love the treatment of everything, because it's all done with respect."[35]

Respect. This is what Americans of Arab origin want—to be projected on TV screens as others are, no worse, no better. Image makers seeking to eradicate images of enmity should seriously contemplate the following conversation between the alien father and son in "Earthbound."

"Why do they [the police] hate us, so?" asks the boy.
"I guess because we're . . . different," says the father.
"Just because somebody's different doesn't mean they have to hate 'em. It's stupid!" contests the boy.

"It's been stupid for a long time," concedes the father.

No one knows when the producers of fantasies will begin to understand that just because someone may be perceived as different, they should not prompt viewers to "hate 'em." After all, "it's stupid" to denigrate peoples because of religion, color, ancestry, or country of birth. The ultimate quest should be an image of the Arab as neither saint nor devil but as a fellow human being, with all the potential and frailty that that condition implies.

As Jeffrey Katzenberg, former Disney chairman, says: "Each of us in Holly-wood has the opportunity to assume individual responsibility for creating films (and TV shows, too, for that matter) that elevate rather than denigrate . . ., that shed light rather than dwell in darkness, that aim for the highest common denominator rather than the lowest."[36]

Disney Chairman Michael Eisner echoes Katzenberg's commitment to quality. "I'm very responsible," he told critic Ken Auletta. "And I think our company is very responsible. I would never make a movie that I would not allow my ten-year-old son to go to."[37]

Eisner's and Katzenberg's rhetoric notwithstanding, Professor Joanne Brown of Drake University believes that "Aladdin" is "racist." She explains that the Arab villains display "dark-hooded eyes and large hooked noses. Perhaps I am sensitive to this business about noses because I am Jewish," she writes. Brown wonders how she "would feel if Disney Studios created a cartoon based on a Jewish folk tale that portrayed" Jews as "Shylocks," and her "culture so unsympathetically."[38]

The Arab and Muslim stereotype will be canceled provided screen executives put into practice Katzenberg's philosophy and begin striving for the "highest common denominator." Discrimination and cinematic hate may be erased from screens when producers and industry officials present scenarios that elevate and shed light on all people.

CONCLUSION

Openness to change is an American tradition and the strength of our society. As Benjamin Franklin advised, "To get the bad Customs of a Country chang'd and new ones, though better introduc'd, it is necessary first to remove the Prejudices of the People, enlighten their ignorance, and convince them that their Interest will be promoted by the propos'd Changes; and this is not the work of a Day."[39]

Franklin's words take on added meaning when contemplating the Arab and Muslim stereotype. History teaches us that no one benefits when people are continuously denigrated. Regrettably, we fail to comprehend that when one ethnic or minority group is degraded, we all suffer. Industry professionals have a Promethean role, as they possess the ability to crush damaging caricatures, to shape sensibilities, and to constructively ignite hearts and minds. One such professional who has spoken out is writer-producer Ted Flicker. In his 1988 letter published in the newsletters of the Writers' Guild and Screen Actors' Guild, Flicker, identifying himself as an American Jew, writes: "Arabs are portrayed as crazy billionaires, terrorists, devious voluptuaries, barbaric white slavers, etc., ad nauseam. Dear fellow writers, on behalf of my Arab cousins, I say to you, think before you write that Arab." Adds Flicker, "I think honor requires that we, the makers of our nation's myths, consider the plight of these people . . . and help get rid of the Arab stereotype."[40]

Flicker is not the only television insider to speak out against bigotry. Other TV professionals are concerned about Arab and Muslim stereotypes. In 1980, while being interviewed for my book *The TV Arab*, the producer Alan Rafkin told me: "When I see a Jew portrayed as Shylock, I want to cry. So I know how an Arab feels when he is described as a killer."[41] Recently, in a personal note to this writer, critic Jeffrey Wells expressed some optimism. He wrote that most writers he knows "feel that towel-head villains are a tired cliche." During the summer of 1994 screenwriter J. F. Lawton told him that "the wild-eyed Arab villains in 'True Lies' felt like a joke. They'd already been the villains in 'Hot Shots.' The whole thing has gotten stale."[42]

And in *Entertainment Weekly*, Wells and Pat H. Broeske pointed out that several upcoming terrorist movies displayed a variety of baddies: a non-Muslim psycho, North Koreans, and effete European curs. Only one film, "Executive Decision," which made its way to movie screens in March 1996, featured Arab terrorists. "Finding workable, hissable villains," attests Wells, "has been a tough chore since the fall of Communism."[43]

This writer contends that finding "hissable villains" is a simple chore. All producers and writers need do is present accurate portraits and offer generic culprits. No one benefits when rogues are repeatedly projected according to race, religion, ethnicity, and/or color.

In spite of Wells's assurances about feature films and Flicker's compassionate plea for equity on television, I remain apprehensive as to whether television entertainment programs will soon cease blemishing Arabs and Muslims. After all, the caricatures have served the industry's selfish interests for nearly half a century. As one who has addressed the TV Arab and Muslim problem for twenty-plus years, I know one thing for certain: image makers promoting the stereotype can no longer use ignorance as an excuse for perpetuating enmity. When slandering Arabs and Muslims, they know exactly what they are doing. Observing the bullheaded image maker cling to his stereotypes reminds me of Peanuts's Linus, stubbornly clenching onto his security blanket. Both Linus and the producer know exactly what they are doing. They know their behavior is all wrong. Yet, they remain adamant, refusing to alter their actions.

Perhaps I am too cynical; perhaps the day will come when TV writers and producers will use dialogue and images that heal emotional wounds, not those that inflict them. Perhaps in lieu of showing US "good" Americans beating up THEM *reel* "bad" Arabs, image makers will one day also project honest-to-goodness, true-to-life Arabs and Muslims that viewers can cheer for, not against. Perhaps biases will eventually be shattered.

The impact of the stereotype and the continued absence of realistic portrayals of America's Arabs and Muslims on TV screens has a telling effect on viewers, especially on children with Arab roots and those embracing Islam. Programmers do not project adequate role models; children are denied opportunities to increase their self-esteem, as they are unable to positively identify with their heritage.

The counsels of common sense and fair play should prevail; no one should be excluded from our rich, cultural mosaic. The time is long overdue for the *real* Arab-American to cease being invisible. He/she should be presented in TV programs honestly and accurately, as a vital part of our country's cultural mainstream.

During the early days of television, comedian Milton Berle eloquently addressed the theme of this chapter. During 1951, when he was at the height of his television career as host of the "Texaco Star Theater," he told fellow comedian Danny Thomas, "There is no room in our profession for prejudice."

No room indeed!

NOTES

1. "Blood, Bread and Poetry: Selected Prose," by Adrienne Rich, cited in Ron Takaki's *A Different Mirror: A History of MultiCultural America* (Boston: Little, Brown, 1993), p. 16.

2. Steven Barboza, *American Jihad* (New York: Doubleday, 1993), p. 9.

3. John Buchan, *Greenmantle* (New York: Oxford University Press, 1993), p. 16.

4. Kadi appearing on "48 Hours," January 30, 1991, CBS-TV.

5. NBC-TV Broadcast Standards and Practices Manual, 1982.

6. "48 Hours," CBS-TV, January 30, 1991.

7. "JAG," December 7, 1995, NBC-TV.

8. "Thunder in Paradise ," a two-part program, TNT, January 29 and February 5, 1996.

9. "Married . . . With Children," July 17, 1994, Channel 2, Savannah, GA.

10. "Married . . . With Children," August 24, 1993, KMOV-TV, St. Louis.

11. "Small Wonder," March 3, 1989, Channel 5, Washington, D.C.

12. Teacher's Workshop, University of Wisconsin, Madison, August 6, 1990.

13. Peter Warg, "Censors Changing Their Toons," *Variety*, October 2-8, 1995, p. 95.

14. "Top Grossers," *Entertainment Weekly*, February 2, 1996, p. 28.

15. Ken Tucker, Review of "Father of the Bride, Part II," *Entertainment Weekly*, December 15, 1995, p. 50.

16. Bill Watterson, *Calvin and Hobbes Tenth Anniversary Book* (Kansas City, MO: Andrews and McMeel, 1995), p. 202.

17. Citation is from Sam Keen's speech, presented at the annual meeting of the Association of American Editorial Cartoonists, San Diego, California, May 15, 1986. For additional information on stereotypical portraits in cartoons, see Keen's excellent text, *Faces of the Enemy* (New York: Harper and Row, 1986).

18. Alfred C. Richard, *The Hispanic Image on the Silver Screen* (Westport, CT: Greenwood Press, 1992), p. 192.

19. *A Rush to Judgment*, a special report on Anti-Muslim/Arab stereotyping, harassment, and hate crimes following the bombing of the Oklahoma City's Alfred Murrah Federal Building, April 19, 1995. (Washington, D.C.: Council on American-Islamic Relations [CAIR], September, 1995).

20. "Jihad in America!" November 27, 1994, PBS-TV.

21. "Eye on America," October 3, 1994, CBS-TV.

22. "The Islamic Bomb," November, 1982, PBS-TV, Channel 9, St. Louis. "Bomb" was first telecast in England on the BBC, August 12, 1981.

23. "The Sword of Islam," January 12, 1988, PBS-TV, Channel 9, St. Louis.

24. "Terrorist on Trial," January 10, 1994, CBS-TV.

25. CAIR, "Action Alert: Denver Mosque Violated," March 24, 1996.

26. Editorial, "It's Racist, but Hey, It's Disney," *The New York Times*, July 14, 1993.

27. Editorial, "The Other Anti-Semitism," *The New Republic*, March 1, 1980, pp. 5-7.

28. "The Jon Stewart Show," February 25, 1995, KMOV-TV, St. Louis.

29. "Twisted Puppet Theater," July 23, 1995, Showtime.

30. "X-Files," May 26, 1995, FOX-TV.

31. "Time Trax," July 15, 1994, FOX-TV.

32. Laila Lalami, " 'Bride' Walks Down the Aisle of Stereotyping," "Counterpunch," *Los Angeles Times*, January 1, 1996.

33. Terrence Beasor, "Stereotypes: A Time-Honored Tradition," "Counterpunch," *Los Angeles Times*, January 8, 1996.

34. Casey Kasem, letter to "Counterpunch," *Los Angeles Times,* January 29, 1996.

35. Frank Bruni, "Disney Did Its Homework on 'Pocahontas.' " *Island Packet*, June 11, 1995, p. 9D.

36. Charles Champlin, "Reflections on the Silver Screen," *Modern Maturity*, June, 1995, p. 23.

37. Ken Auletta, "What They Won't Do?" *The New Yorker*, May 17, 1993, p. 48.

38. Joanne Brown, "Stereotypes Ruin the Fun of Aladdin," *Des Moines Register*, December 22, 1992, p. 12.

39. Franklin citation from *Not the Work of a Day: The Story of the Anti-Defamation League of the B'nai B'rith* (New York: Anti-Defamation League, 1965), p. 1.

40. Prior to addressing the guilds, Ted Flicker gave this writer a copy of his speech. See Shaheen's *Los Angeles Times* essay, "Television Chose to Make the Palestinian America's Bogeyman," January 10, 1988, p. 5.

41. See Rafkin's comments in Jack G. Shaheen, *The TV Arab* (Bowling Green, OH: The Popular Press, 1984), p. 64.

42. Jeffrey Wells's letter to the author, December 2, 1995.

43. Jeffrey Wells and Pat H. Broeske, "The 'Hard Stuff,' " *Entertainment Weekly*, December 1, 1995, pp. 8-9.

IV

Articles by
Media Critics/Journalists

13

Religion and Prime Time Television

Thomas Plate

There is a huge, even daunting anomaly in our media life. It is to be found in the stunning disconnect between the increasing importance of religion in America and its persistently scanty portrayal on prime time television. What's going on here? Does every prime time TV program have to be "Baywatch"? No room in the fall lineup for God?

No one can say that religion isn't in itself vitally important in American life; or that the subject of religion isn't often frighteningly prominent in the news. Consider just some recent headlines: conflicts in the Middle East, fueled by ancient religious hatred; the federal raid on David Koresh's Branch Davidian compound, raising questions not just about eccentric religious cults but the whole uneasy relationship between church and state in America; Pope John Paul II's various foreign visits, always well covered by the news media; and the bombing of the World Trade Center by militant Muslims.

Moreover, beneath the immediacy of the headlines, deep-seated personal religious beliefs and powerful religious movements swirl in the subterranean regions of American culture, now and then coming up to the top with all the drama of a huge whale surfacing for air. Even the superficial evidence of religion's enduring importance is impressive: In New York alone, for example, at least 3,500 places of worship serve the city's 7.3 million inhabitants.

Increasingly, more attention is being paid to the topic of religion in some quarters of the news media. Wise newspapers have religion sections or religion pages; some have one or two full-time staffers assigned to that beat; and some organizations, such as ABC News, have a full-time religious-issues correspondent on staff. For all this, most thoughtful news executives would not argue that the news side of television has done an exemplary job of covering religion. CBS News anchor Dan Rather has admitted that religion is "constantly under-reported" by the news media.

But compared to the entertainment side, the news divisions have dealt with their responsibility in this area almost religiously. On prime time TV, religion is conspicuous only by its absence. No wonder that so many leading civic, not to mention religious, leaders are alarmed by this disconnect and wish, fervently and sincerely, that prime time did more with religious topics.

Their sincere alarm arises from the fear that an absence of religion from the nation's major medium of communication bodes ill for the quality of that communication; that such an absence only serves to deepen, however inadvertently, the nation's excessive secularization; and that the spectacular paucity of religious story lines and religious values on prime time TV works to embed secular values in the general culture that are manifestly inadequate to meet the moral and ethical challenges of our time.

That level of alarm, which seems to mount with each fall season's programming announcement, raises important and complicated questions. Perhaps TV should do more with religion. Then again, perhaps not. Perhaps it is a mistake to ask prime time TV to attempt to fulfill a cultural responsibility for which it is preternaturally unsuited.

Consider the nature of religion and the nature of television. Religion emphasizes commitment and passion and, in the end, soulful privacy; television is a cool medium for a mass audience. To the extent that religion appears on the air at any time in the neighborhood of prime time hours, it's in the form of televangelism made famous, and often notorious, by media personalities like Robert Schuller, Jimmy Swaggart, Oral Roberts, and Billy Graham. Is this the kind of prime time television programming that those who are alarmed have in mind?

Professor Neil Postman put the issue this way some ten years ago, "On television, religion, like everything else, is presented, quite simply and without apology, as an entertainment. Everything that makes religion an historic, profound and sacred human activity is stripped away; there is no ritual, no dogma, no tradition, no theology, and above all, no sense of spiritual transcendence. On these shows, the preacher is tops. God comes out as second banana."[1]

If the Crystal Cathedral or Oral Roberts University is not what most of the critics have in mind for prime time TV, what else could be wanted? A prime time series? (Subbing, say, a new show called "Popewatch" for "Baywatch"?!!) Excuse the unrelenting and admitted cynicism if you can, but it is my judgment that the only thing worse for America than religion topics not dealt with on prime time TV would be religion topics dealt with during prime time.

The problem is not so much with religion as with television. It is a medium for the entertainment of the masses. It is not a spiritual medium ideally suited for inner reflection and communication with a Higher Being.

Wisely, prime time television, which generally knows what it is doing, has tended to avoid the topic much in the same way that people tend not to be foolish enough to try to dance to Beethoven. It's just not a good mix. But for the vitally important topic of religion, I would argue, it's worse than a bad mix; it could prove a disastrous one.

The very essence of religion in America is not homogenization but unlimited freedom of expression. There is not one Christian faith but many; there is not one Jewish school of religion but several. And while America was founded by statesmen and leaders who were often practicing Christians, the constitution they so brilliantly and astutely wrote was explicit in prohibiting the founding of any state religion; thus in America many Eastern, non-Christian religions flourish, as well as Judaism and countless forms of Christianity.

The strength of American religion is in its diversity. But prime time television, as contradistinguished from an ever-increasing number of niche-nestling cable stations, cannot handle that level of diversity, nuance, or spiritual intimacy. Nor can it handle any degree whatsoever of interior spirituality. That's why religion belongs in the churches and synagogues and mosques, and in the hearts and minds of Americans, not on prime time television. More religious programming on prime time TV might just prove a cure worse than the disease. I say: Avoid it at all costs.

Always remember: Fools rush in where angels fear to tread.

NOTE

1. Neil Postman, *Amusing Ourselves to Death* (New York: Penguin Books, 1985), pp. 116-117.

Hollywood Makes Room for Religion

Michael Medved

Prominent figures in today's Hollywood have explored a multitude of exotic spiritual paths in their ongoing quest for personal fulfillment. Most recently, however, more and more members of the entertainment elite have followed that quest to the most startling and unexpected exploration of them all—the rediscovery of traditional Christianity and Judaism.

While it would be somewhat premature to declare Hollywood a fortress of spiritual strength, or a vibrant new center for old-time religion, the recent changes in the show business community are both striking and significant. Those who adhere to mainstream Western religions no longer function as a persecuted minority in the entertainment industry, while fervently faithful Christians and Jews have assumed new positions of prominence.

Consider, for a moment, some of the elements that the most popular movie release of 1994 ("The Lion King") shares with the year's top-rated TV series ("Home Improvement"). Both these phenomenally successful projects appeal to broad family audiences to try to affirm wholesome values of responsibility, integrity, and respect. Both projects originated, appropriately enough, at divisions of the Walt Disney Company. And both happen to be produced by outspoken and deeply committed evangelical Christians.

Don Hahn, producer of "The Lion King" as well as the similarly beloved "Beauty and the Beast," is a lifelong churchgoer who addressed the 1992 convention of the National Religious Broadcasters and spoke movingly about the impact of Christ and faith on his life and work.

David McFadzean, executive producer and co-creator of "Home Improvement,"

Reprinted from *The American Enterprise*, a Washington-based magazine of politics, business, and culture (1-800-596-2319).

"Thunder Alley," and other hugely profitable TV ventures, is deeply involved in the life of his neighborhood church and the larger religious community. Before making his way to the cutthroat world of big-time television, he and his partners worked together in "The Lamb's Players," a theatrical troupe of born-again Christians dedicated to using their creative gifts for spreading God's word.

Hahn and McFadzean may be the most visible of the new breed of religious believers in Tinseltown, but they by no means stand alone. Scores of other writers, producers, directors, executives, and stars are currently trying to keep the faith in the traditionally inhospitable world of Hollywood—including Barry Weiss and David Steinberg, co-producers of "The Pagemaster," the holiday-season family movie from 20th Century Fox that combined animation, live action, and the acting talents of Macaulay Culkin and Christopher Lloyd. Weiss and Steinberg, a pair of Orthodox Jewish kids from the same neighborhood in Chicago, ran their movie as the first *shomer shabbos* (Sabbath observant) production in Hollywood history— permitting no work between sundown on Friday and full dark on Saturday night.

There are others:

Ken Wales, the former Disney studio vice-president and producer of "Islands in the Stream" and other feature films, is a tirelessly idealistic "PK" ("preacher's kid") whose single-minded dedication finally paid off in his long struggle to dramatize the cherished Christian novel *Christy*. The resulting TV series which debuted in 1994 recreated the struggles of a dedicated missionary teacher working in the remote reaches of Appalachia at the turn of the century. With its emphasis on courage, faith, and the power of prayer and decency, "Christy" drew more supportive mail than any series in the history of CBS.

Steve Spira, the universally popular head of business affairs for Warner Brothers, is a strictly observant Jew who happens to be the first major Hollywood executive to wear a *yarmulke* (skullcap) every day at work.

Martha Williamson, executive producer and writer of the CBS show "Touched By an Angel," is a passionate Christian with a background working for Carol Burnett and Joan Rivers. Her series dramatizes the adventures of a beautiful angel who comes to earth every week to comfort or inspire various characters in moments of crisis.

Coleman Luck, co-creator and producer of "Quantum Leap," "Gabriel's Fire," and other television shows, is also one of the leaders of Inter-Mission, an organization of more than 1,700 entertainment industry professionals who, according to the group's mission statement, share "a love of Jesus Christ, a passion for excellence, and a desire to effect moral change on popular culture."

Many of these people have worked in the industry for years, struggling to maintain the difficult balance between career and faith. They universally report that the most important recent changes in the nature of that struggle involve a new ability to discuss religious commitment with their non-religious colleagues without feeling embarrassment or discomfort. The small community of believers in the entertainment industry has developed a center of gravity: those who are active in church or synagogue life and are now too numerous, and too successful, to be trivialized or marginalized.

An acclaimed and undeniably flourishing professional like David McFadzean can wield an industry-wide impact through the force of his example. For one thing, a few respected role models who manage to combine religious faith and Hollywood success can inspire many others with religious inclinations to "come out of the closet"—while leading still others to consider religious ideas and practices more seriously and sympathetically. If the committed Jews and Christians who are now taking their place among the entertainment establishment achieve nothing else, they have succeeded in helping to destroy some of the tired old industry stereotypes about what it means to be religious. For all those who cross paths with an unfailingly genial, urbane, and sophisticated Christian artist like Ken Wales, it's simply impossible to maintain the nasty notion that all evangelicals are joyless, witless, yahoos with clothes from K-mart and ideas from the *National Enquirer*.

In fact, by changing the image of religious commitment within the industry, Hollywood's more fervent believers are helping to bring about a quiet revolution in the way that movies and TV present spiritual themes and personalities on screen.

Nearly everyone who monitors the industry's treatment of organized faith has taken note of the recent change. Last year, for instance, Monsignor Francis Manistalco, a spokesman for the National Council of Bishops, flatly stated that "religion is being treated more seriously in today's TV." He went on to express gratitude for the networks' new tendency toward "showing religion as influential in people's lives." Meanwhile, the Media Research Center, a scientifically grounded television monitoring service in Alexandria, Virginia, released the results of a comprehensive study of all prime time shows broadcast on the four major networks during 1993. Their report, "Faith in a Box: Entertainment Television on Religion," issued in March 1994, concluded: "When it comes to prime time and religion, matters are more balanced than they were a few years ago."

Despite the continued presence of many gratuitous insults on sitcoms, or highly negative characterizations of clergy in prime time dramas and TV movies, television offered more countervailing positive portrayals than it had at any time in recent years. For instance, in the final season of NBC's "L.A. Law," the show's prestigious law firm welcomed a bright, idealistic, drop-dead gorgeous attorney (Alexandra Powers) who also happened to be prime time's first born-again Christian character. Over at ABC, even the "Roseanne" show introduced a story line in which one of the main character's children began attending church regularly—and appeared to be a better person because of it.

The situation in feature films is similar. Hollywood's relentless religion-bashing of the last fifteen years (which I have documented at length in several articles and my 1992 book *Hollywood vs. America*) has become more understated and infrequent. While a few recent films have recycled the old, one-sided anti-religious stereotypes (like the murderous Christian prison warden in the "Shawshank Redemption"), many other movies offered surprisingly affectionate and respectful treatments of organized faith. In 1993, the Oscar-nominated "Shadowlands" told the sad but romantic story of the late-in-life marriage of the great Christian writer

C. S. Lewis, and even quoted Lewis on the importance of prayer.

"Rudy," an uplifting true story about an undersized working-class kid determined to make the Notre Dame football team, featured the most admirable on-screen characterization of a Catholic priest since the death of Bing Crosby. More recently, Kevin Costner's character quoted the Bible and repeatedly affirmed his faith in the heartfelt but little-seen melodrama "The War," while the wildly popular "Forrest Gump" contained numerous (and generally affirmative) references to religion and Divine Providence. The 1994 remake of "Miracle on 34th Street" went even further with its enthusiastic endorsement of organized faith. When the main character Kriss Kringle (Sir Richard Attenborough) declares, "If you can't believe, you'll live the rest of your life dominated by doubt," he's not simply talking about faith in Santa Claus. This becomes clear in the climactic courtroom scene, where the judge gives an inspiring little speech (not present in the original 1947 film) on the deeper meaning of the words "In God We Trust."

Of course, these pro-faith messages in major Hollywood films or TV shows don't necessarily mean that the producers suddenly found their way to profound religious passion; the profit motive is still more important in the entertainment business than the prophet motive. If they throw in a religious character in an established TV series like "Roseanne" or "L.A. Law" (or "Picket Fences" or "Northern Exposure," for that matter) you can assume it's a bid for ratings rather than a statement of faith.

Savvy television or movie producers can read the same surveys the rest of us do—showing, for example, that 75% of Americans say they pray "regularly" while 82% believe that the Bible is either the "actual" or "the inspired word of God" (this according to the National Opinion Research Center). In this context, repeated attempts to classify religious believers as crooked or crazy make no sense—especially in view of the consistent failure of projects that contain such denigrating characters, and the surprising success of those films ("Chariots of Fire," "Driving Miss Daisy," "Sister Act") that take a more affirmative view of organized faith.

Nevertheless, the presence of devoted Jews and Christians in key positions in the entertainment industry has greatly aided the shift to more supportive on-screen treatment of religious themes and characters. This body of believers provides an invaluable resource for an industry that seems eager to connect with the religious sentiments of the general public but often has no idea where to start.

Like all other creative artists, TV and movie producers work most effectively when reflecting aspects of life that they know firsthand. It is no accident that the acclaimed (though recently canceled) NBC series "Against the Grain," about the loving, church-going family of a small-town football coach in Texas, originated with talented Christian producer Dave Johnson; nor is it a coincidence that "A Stranger Among Us," a murder mystery that offered a glowing (and surprisingly detailed) view of life among the fervently religious Hasidim of Brooklyn, began with a screenplay by Robert Avrech, a committed member of California's largest Orthodox Jewish congregation.

Even "Schindler's List," perhaps the most universally praised motion picture of our time, owes some of its religious sensibility to the personal journey of its creator. The film begins and ends with lovingly rendered Jewish rituals, the first time that Steven Spielberg ever made serious reference to his heritage in any of his films. This may stem in part from the filmmaker's recent experience studying Torah with his wife, Kate Capshaw, to complete her conversion to Judaism under Orthodox auspices.

To encourage such individual commitments, and to generate the continued momentum of Hollywood's quiet religious revival, several organizations have sprung up. Inter-Mission, founded in 1987, is easily the largest and most visible of them, with its nearly 2,000 members, its regular educational and social events centered at Hollywood's First Presbyterian Church, and its popular and critically praised Actors Co-op productions of faith-affirming stage plays. Another impressive group of Evangelical Christians has gathered around the efforts of the sophisticated and charismatic Dr. Larry Poland. His MasterMedia International sponsors "key man" luncheon meetings that provide an unpublicized, informal network for religiously committed executives in all the major studios and TV networks.

Meanwhile, the Los Angeles Film Studies Center works with students from Christian colleges, providing them with a grounding on issues of media and values, helping them secure coveted internships with leading production companies and easing their path into full-time work in the industry. Mormons have also begun to create a network within the show business community; their organization of more than two hundred members, Association of Latter-day Media Artists (ALMA), meets several times a year.

Among the disproportionate number of industry professionals who claim Jewish ancestry, the upsurge in religious activity is even more dramatic. The membership in the Synagogue for the Performing Arts has swelled to more than nine hundred and, more importantly, that nondenominational congregation has taken a decisive turn toward religious traditionalism. Its new rabbi, the Orthodox-ordained Joseph Telushkin, is the author of the recent best seller *Jewish Literacy* and a passionate, eloquent advocate of Sabbath observance and kosher dietary laws. On October 7, 1994, he welcomed to his pulpit Kirk Douglas, who made a most remarkable declaration of faith. Having "for a long time drifted away from Judaism," Douglas reported that he had recently reconsidered the importance of religion. "That is when I started to think that we should thank those pious, black-hatted, bearded Jews—for keeping Judaism alive for so long. They understood something very deep that we more secular types never learned, or forgot if we did: God gave us the Torah—and that made us the conscience of the world."

Until recently, few among Hollywood's religious community would have spoken publicly in such terms. Today, several organizations work to reach the entertainment industry's many unaffiliated Jews with a more traditional Jewish message. The Jerusalem-based educational institution Aish HaTorah (The Fire of Torah) opened a branch in Los Angeles ten years ago and has made major inroads into the entertainment community. Pacific Jewish Center, the outreach-oriented congregation with which I've been affiliated for eighteen years, counts among its members and alumni numerous producers, actors, writers, executives, and agents. One alumnus, a successful young screenwriter named Jeff Schechter, has recently assembled a group of more than three dozen Orthodox writers who intend to meet regularly to share ideas and encouragement.

In light of their deep differences in theology and style, the burgeoning Jewish and Christian groups in Hollywood have as yet made no formal attempt to work together, but their individual members cooperate on worthy endeavors nearly every day. On the most profound and personal level, religious Jews and Christians manage to inspire one another, and to find significant areas of agreement in the struggle for basic decency and the defense of traditional values in the popular culture. Since secularists are still the vast majority within the entertainment industry, it's natural for believers of any description to feel a sense of fellowship and common purpose that cuts across sectarian boundaries.

The behind-the-scenes experience on the CBS show "Christy" offers a case in point. Christian producer Ken Wales initially worried that his Jewish co-producer Barney Rosenzweig might want to eliminate some of the script references to prayer and faith. But Rosenzweig—who had begun studying traditional Judaism several years before with the rabbis at Aish HaTorah, and who had already created prime time's first outspokenly Orthodox character (the selfless, dedicated public defender on "The Trials of Rosie O'Neill")—felt entirely comfortable with the religious themes in "Christy," and he joined with Wales in persuading the predictably timid network to retain them.

Out of such small victories are revolutions made. While most Americans have hardly noticed, key institutions and personalities of popular culture have begun developing a notably more hospitable attitude toward organized religion. Hollywood's current status still leaves vast room for improvement, but an exhilarating spirit of change—if not outright rebirth and revival—is already in the air.

15

A Cacophony of Prime Time Religions?

Theodore Baehr

Religion is alive and well on network, prime time, fiction television, but it is not the predominantly Christian faith of our founding fathers or an intimate relationship with the God of the patriarchs. Instead, it is a cacophony of ill-conceived religions such as materialism, consumerism, eroticism, hedonism, naturalism, humanism, cynicism, stoicism, the cult of violence (which used to pay homage to the war-god Mars), and a multitude of other modern variations on pagan practices which now vie for renewed homage on prime time entertainment television. These religions, many of which can trace their roots back to long-discredited ancient cults, have their rituals, beliefs, values, signs, significations, metaphysics, cosmologies, ontologies, epistemologies, and ultimate meanings played out night after night, program after program (and commercial after commercial) with ritualistic regularity. Thus, on any given night on prime time fiction television, we may find happy Buddhist monks hawking athletic gear, or Hollywood stars touting the virtues of astrology.

DEEPEST FEELINGS AND ULTIMATE CONCERNS

Of course, materialists might quibble that their beliefs exclude anything but the natural, and Buddhists might intone that they are non-theistic, but as philosopher Ludwig Feuerbach reveals, even "atheism . . . is the secret of religion itself; [in] that religion itself, not indeed on the surface, but fundamentally, not in intention or according to its own supposition, but in its heart, in its essence, believes in nothing else than the truth and divinity of human nature."[1] Feuerbach's contention may rile theists, but it does grasp the essence of many anthropocentric religions.

Furthermore, with the fall of the Berlin Wall, most pundits will admit that Marxism, the "ultimate humanism" as Marx called it, "is a religion," as Austrian econo-

mist Joseph A. Schumpeter astutely concluded in 1942.[2] Schumpeter explained,
"To the believer it presents, first, a system of ultimate ends that embody the meaning of life and are absolute standards by which to judge events and actions; and,
secondly, a guide to those ends which implies a plan of salvation and the indication of the evil from which mankind, or a chosen section of mankind, is to be
saved."

For some in the dream world of the mass media of entertainment "sex is the
mysticism of materialism and the only possible religion in a materialistic society,"
as the prominent British broadcaster Malcolm Muggeridge incisively concluded.[3]
For others, harking back to the rituals of ancient cultures of the Mediterranean
with their temples of sport, "modern body building is ritual, religion, sport, art,
and science, awash in Western chemistry and mathematics. Defying nature, it sur-
passes it," explained critic Camille Paglia.[4]

For millions, in a manner not too dissimilar from pagan sacrifices, the following words of novelist E. L. Doctorow are apropos: "[M]urders are exciting and lift
people into a heart-beating awe as religion is supposed to do, after seeing one in
the street, young couples will go back to bed and make love, people will cross
themselves and thank God for the gift of their stuporous lives, old folks will talk to
each other over cups of hot water with lemon because murders are enlivened sermons to be analyzed and considered and relished, they speak to the timid of the
dangers of rebellion, murders are perceived as momentary descents of God and so
provide joy and hope and righteous satisfaction to parishioners, who will talk about
them for years afterward to anyone who will listen."[5]

An even more prominent player in the pantheon of media religions is television
itself. If, as British playwright J. M. Barrie concludes, "one's religion is whatever
he is most interested in,"[6] or, as theologian Paul Tillich explains, "your god is that
reality which elicits from you your deepest feelings and ultimate concerns" and
"religion is the state of being grasped by an ultimate concern, a concern which
qualifies all other concerns as preliminary and which itself contains the answer to
the question of a meaning of our life,"[7] then prime time entertainment television
itself has become a religion for many viewers and many of those employed in the
entertainment industry.

THE FAITH OF OUR FATHERS

In spite of the crowded religious bazaar on prime time entertainment television,
a growing number of Americans are raising their voices to bemoan the lack of
religion on prime time entertainment television. In most cases, these critics of the
culture of television do not refer to the cacophony of anthropocentric religious
fervor on the tube but rather to the absence of the faith of our fathers that is still the
faith of the millions of Christians (85.6% of the U.S. population calls themselves
Christians according to a 1991 CUNY survey) and Jews whose faith is premised
on a personal relationship with the Creator God. These followers of the theocentric
or revealed religions, which are based on the unique actions of God reaching out to

man,[8] stand in philosophic and theological opposition to the anthropocentric, non-revealed religions so prevalent on television, which are based on man searching for God, godliness, or meaning in life.[9] They stand in opposition even though the theocentrists applaud the anthropocentrist's search for God as a step in the right direction toward finding out the truth that can set man free from his solipsism. Research has shown that theocentric religions are under-represented on prime time entertainment television, although there has been a significant increase in their presence in the last few years in popular programs such as "Christy," "Touched by an Angel," and even "Dr. Quinn, Medicine Woman."

In this regard, a 1990 study commissioned by the American Family Association found that the religious side (referring to the theocentric Christian and Jewish religions) of people's lives is rarely included in the fictional world of TV. In the study, three researchers analyzed one hundred episodes of prime time network programs appearing on ABC, CBS, NBC, and Fox during one month. The investigators conducted a systematic content analysis which examined the religious and spiritual behaviors of characters as well as the appearance of religious images, artifacts, and rituals such as churches, crosses, and prayer services.

Of the 1,462 speaking characters in the study, only 81 had a religious affiliation. Of all characters on TV, 94.57% had no discernible religious affiliation. Religious behaviors, in most cases, were very brief statements such as "Thank God!" after a close call. In over 50% of the occurrences, religious behaviors were negative.

The AFA study suggested that religion is a rather invisible institution on fictional network TV. Overall, the message being presented about religion by network TV is that it is not very important because it is rarely a factor in the lives of the characters depicted or in the society in which they are portrayed.

A 1995 study by the Media Research Center found that prime time television's treatment of religion (again defined in terms of the theocentric religions) had improved somewhat from 1993 to 1994. In entertainment programming, the number of portrayals of religion in prime time more than doubled from 1993 to 1994 (116 to 253), even though the amount of hours of original prime time programming increased only slightly (1,674.5 to 1,716). Overall, positive depictions outnumbered negative ones by almost two-to-one (44% to 23%). In 1993, negatives were in the majority by the same ratio (56% to 28%). Shows singled out for their positive treatment of religion were "Christy" and "Touched by an Angel" (CBS), "Thunder Alley" (ABC), and "L.A. Law" and "Homicide: Life on the Street" (NBC).

PRESUPPOSITIONS

It is important to note that many of those on the other side of the theological divide often contend that there is a lack of religion on prime time television either because they do not understand the meaning of the term or because they do not want to admit that their own particular worldview has religious implications. It is also important to keep in mind in the midst of this debate that many Christians will point out that their faith is not a religion in the sense of required modes of behavior and worship, but rather a dynamic personal relationship with the living God. These theologically astute, orthodox Christians will often be more concerned with the redemptive and gracious aspects of fictional television, rather than the trappings of religion such as prayer, crucifixes, and church scenes, although it can be justifiably argued that these trappings are important as significants of a personal faith.

WHOSE VALUES?

In any event, there are several salient reasons why many Americans are concerned if Christianity and Judaism or the cults of violence, consumerism, and materialism are portrayed in the lives of the characters on television. These concerns need to be addressed by television executives, producers, and talent before they are swept up in a conflagration much more intense than the current culture wars.

At a very basic level, many believers feel alienated from the culture they witness on television, which they may view as a window on the world or at least as a distorted mirror of life. This was not so thirty years ago when Timothy prayed before going to find "Lassie" and a theocentric faith was often at least a small part of the fabric of the lives of many of the characters on television. Now, the viewer finds most television characters alien with their lack of faith and often anti-Christian attitudes. For example, the American Family Association, mirroring the concerns of millions of Americans, expressed shock and dismay when in one episode of "Roseanne," instead of a prayer before dinner, Roseanne complained profanely about the possibility that her son is going to church.

Quite often, this pronounced lack of faith of television's fictional characters is highly unrealistic when compared to the lives of most Americans. For instance, in the many programs where the key characters are involved in extremely dangerous and life-threatening situations, they do everything but pray. There may be no "atheists in fox holes" in the real world, but there seems to be an overabundance of people who curse God in the face of extreme danger in the fictional world of the mass media of entertainment. This reaction to life-threatening situations appears not only unrealistic but blasphemous to the 60% of the American people who go to church at least once a month, and especially to the 40%, or approximately 102 million Americans, who make it to church to worship Jesus Christ every week, according to the Gallup Organization.

Many of the remaining 26.5% of Americans who may not frequent their local church on a consistent basis but claim to be believers also complain in Gallup and other national polls about the profane attitude of most television characters toward God. According to the "Associated Press Media General Survey" released in May of 1989, 80% of the American people object to cursing on television and in the movies. According to a more recent *USA Weekend* survey of 65,142 television viewers released on June 2, 1995, 97% of audience members are very concerned about cursing on television.

Perhaps television writers, talent, and executives do not realize that very few Americans curse with any regularity unless they are characters in the mass media of entertainment or one of the denizens of the entertainment industry in Hollywood or New York. According to an intensive, comprehensive study entitled "Cursing in America" conducted by Professor Timothy Jay (whom the *Wall Street Journal* calls the "preeminent scholar of profanity") at Massachusetts State College, only 7% of Americans curse on the job and only 12% curse in their leisure time.

A corollary concern of millions of Americans who complain about the lack of revealed religion on television is the conflict between the values being portrayed on television and their own personal values. Values are a byproduct of one's religion in the comprehensive sense that one's values are determined by one's worldview, even if one is an atheist or a humanist. For those who hold to a theocentric faith, values such as "Thou shalt not kill" are prescribed by God and must therefore be observed, or there are consequences. For those who believe that there is no higher, benevolent "other" and believe that they are the measure of all things, anything goes, and they are hard pressed to explain what makes their own values better than someone else's such as Hitler, Stalin, or other famous megalomaniacs.

Furthermore, if there is no higher authority and the individual is the measure of all things, then there are no consequences except perhaps a clash of values with human beings whose metaphysical musings have led them to other conclusions. As Henry Wadsworth Longfellow stated, "morality without religion [in a theocentric sense] is only a kind of dead reckoning—an endeavor to find our place on a cloudy sea by measuring the distance we have run, but without any observation of the heavenly bodies."[10] Or, as more stridently stated by the English statesman John Selden, "he that has not religion [again, in a theocentric sense] to govern his morality, is not a dram better than my mastiff-dog; so long as you stroke him, and please him, and do not pinch him, he will play with you as finely as may be; he is a very good, moral mastiff; but if you hurt him, he will fly in your face and tear out your throat."[11]

In a 1995 Gallup poll for the Catholic Communication Campaign, the majority of Americans in every age group said that it is "very or somewhat important that movies they see reflect their own moral and ethical values." A June 8, 1995, *USA Today*/CNN/Gallup poll reported that 65% of the American people feel that "the entertainment industry is seriously out of touch with the values of the American people." Aside from the paramount admonition to not take the name of God in vain which was discussed above, revealed values as set forth in the Bible emphasize loving your neighbor and, as a consequence, refraining from murder, theft, and false witness. In contrast, that which is valued on television is often selfishness featuring revenge, violence, and deception as a means to having some pumped-up brute force triumph over some lesser, though perhaps more sinister, elements.

CULTURE WARS

This conflict of values has been characterized as a culture war because television has been a primary teacher of our youth, and parents are concerned about what their children are being taught. A 1994 *USA Today* poll found that over 80%

of the American people believe that the biggest problem facing society today is the breakdown of morality, and a vast majority of those people believe that the mass media of entertainment are responsible for this breakdown. A poll of children aged ten to sixteen conducted by Children Now found that 62% of children believe that television influences their behavior to some degree. Even 87% of the top media executives believe that the violence in the media contributes to the violence in society, according to a 1994 UCLA/*U.S. News and World Report* survey of three thousand top executives.

A 1995 *New York Times* poll found that although the average adult in the United States watches television for more than four hours a day, a little more than half of the adults polled could not think of a single good thing to say about television, or about movies or popular music. In contrast, nine out of ten of those interviewed could think of something bad to say about the mass media of entertainment, with a large proportion mentioning too much sex, violence, and vulgar language, and a smaller percentage citing bias and stupidity.

Furthermore, the *New York Times* study confirmed that many Americans believe there is a direct connection between the fictional world on television to which young people are exposed and the way young people behave in real life. Approximately half of those surveyed believe that portrayals of sex and violence on television, in movies, and in music lyrics contribute significantly to whether teenagers become sexually active or violent. Another quarter said they believe such portrayals contribute to some degree. Only a fifth expressed the belief that the portrayals of sex and violence in popular culture have "little" or "no" influence on the behavior of teenagers.

Asked to name for themselves what is most to blame for teenage violence, 21% of those polled volunteered "television," 6% blamed "the media" more generally, and 4% cited movies. Altogether, 33% of those polled named some aspect of the mass media of entertainment, making it the most often cited cause. Another 33% cited some aspect of family life, including lack of parental discipline and family breakdown, both of which many also link to the mass media of entertainment's influence on culture.

The *New York Times* poll, which surveyed 1,209 adults, found little difference between the opinions of parents and those of adults in general.

However, according to the *Times* study, members of the entertainment industry argue that the concerns about mass entertainment's impact are overstated and that no clear-cut connection has ever been demonstrated between the violence children see on television and the crimes they commit on the streets. The *Times* points out that it is true that many of the studies on the topic have failed to come up with a strong statistical correlation between what children watch and what they do, but that among social scientists there is a broad consensus that there is at least an indirect relationship between popular culture and behavior. Furthermore, the *Times* noted that the television industry implicitly believes this to be the case since television executives make the case to advertisers that buying air time to promote their products will boost their sales.

Most of the parents interviewed said that they saw direct evidence of the connection between the mass media of entertainment and behavior, noting that their children imitated behavior and language they picked up from television, movies, and radio. In this regard, the *Times* had an interesting response from one of the parents interviewed:

"It's the way they talk and the way they view life in general," reported 41-year-old Denise O'Hara of Roswell, Georgia, the mother of two teenage boys. "They say, 'I'm going to kill you,' like it's O.K., like it's nothing. They don't understand that when you kill someone, that's it, they're gone. It's like 'Oh cool, oh neat, watching this is great.'"

Many parents understand and see the influence of prime time television on the most obscure aspects of their children's behavior. Parents know all too well that it is hard to argue with the little three-year-old boy in Tulsa, Oklahoma, who insists that his name is Bruce Wayne (because secretly he is really Batman) and throws a fit every time his mother calls him by his given name.

PRIMARY TEACHER

If teaching demands presenting information, repeating information, and reinforcing information, then television may well be classified as a primary teacher of our youth.

By the time they are seventeen years old, the average American youth has watched 17,000 to 33,000 hours of television,[12] including 200,000 to 400,000 sexual references and acts (which include everything from vamping, to touching, to kissing, to fondling, to fornication), [13] 100,000 to 200,000 acts of violence, and 17,000 to 33,000 murders. The same child goes to school for 11,000 hours.[14] Clearly, television has the educational edge in terms of the "class" time.

According to Dr. Victor Cline at the University of Utah, 92% of teenagers under the age of eighteen have seen extreme pornographic sex and violence, 64% want to copy what they see, and over 40% do copy what they see. A 1994 study reported in the *Journal of the American Medical Association* found that 30% of young offenders behind bars said that they were consciously copying what they saw in movies and on television. According to the California Justice Department, 21% of teenage crime is directly copied from what the teenagers see in movies and on television, right down to the minute gory details. A study from Children Now shows that 64% of teenagers believe that their friends copy what they see on television.

Dr. Thomas Redechi, former director of the National Coalition on Television Violence, has concluded that the evidence is now irrefutable that the mass media of entertainment influence behavior. Therefore, it is for good reason that many parents question what television is teaching our children about sex, violence, and religion.

For many reasons, not the least of which is the desire to capture an audience, television programs and movies quite often feature the worship of the sex goddess or the god of war with their attendant self-destructive values. According to renowned historians Oswald Spengler and Will Durant, such pagan cults laid waste to ancient civilizations,[15] and there is good evidence that they are now corroding our civilization. Although the average viewer may not have studied the consequences of the worship of Astarte in ancient Asia Minor, he is concerned about the consequence of his children watching excessive sex and violence on his television set and does not want his children to be caught up in these cults of self-destruction.

REEL WORLD

Of course, there are those parents who believe that their children need to be exposed to "life" and other parents who don't care about the values taught by the tube. The problem with the first attitude is that television is not cinema verite (which, by the way, never succeeded because people watch television and movies most often to escape the reality of their everyday lives). Television does not portray reality or life but a particular and intentionally emotive perspective on reality. For instance, the National Coalition on Television Violence compared the number of violent murders on "Miami Vice" (about five per half-hour) with the number of murders the average policeman in Miami witnesses during his tenure on the police force (most often, none), and found that "Miami Vice" had little relation to the reality of life in Miami.

Furthermore, with regard to exposing children to life or reality, the great psychologist Jean Piaget noted that an important difference between man and animals is that an animal has to stick its foot in a trap to find out that it is a trap, whereas a man can learn from secondary sources. Thus, a child does not have to be exposed to murder to know that murder is wrong. If we had to experience everything that we learned, civilization would stall, and society might well be reduced to barbarism.

GROWING OPPOSITION

The good news is that children don't want to be abandoned to the television set and object to the ritual worship of sex and violence on television. A 1992 MTv poll found that 92% of MTv's audience wanted less sex and violence. A majority of teenagers polled by Children Now in 1994 felt the same way.

Furthermore, adults are becoming increasingly concerned about what their children are watching. In two separate 1995 polls, Americans told the entertainment industry that they are very concerned about sex, violence, and profanity on television, and in movies and music lyrics. A *USA Weekend* survey, which included responses from over 65,000 viewers, focused on television. Another *USA Today/ CNN/Gallup* poll dealt with broader entertainment industry issues. This latter survey of 65,142 viewers found that: 96% are very concerned or somewhat concerned about sex on TV; 97% are very or somewhat concerned about vulgar language on

TV; 97% are very or somewhat concerned about violence on TV. Of those polled, 63% feel that the federal government should become involved in restricting sex and violence presented by the entertainment industry, 83% believe that the entertainment industry should make a serious effort to reduce sex and violence in movies and music and on TV, and 68% believe that reducing the amount of sex and violence in movies and music and on TV would significantly improve the moral climate of the USA. Of those polled, 65% feel that the entertainment industry is seriously out of touch with the values of the American people. Almost one-half of those polled believe that the entertainment industry is to blame for exposing children of all ages to sex and violence in movies, music, and on TV, with one-half of those who hold the entertainment industry responsible saying that the mass media of entertainment share responsibility with parents.

In many cases, people are taking this perceived cultural war so seriously that they are turning off broadcast and cable television and relying on videotapes for their entertainment choices. A recent insiders' poll for the television industry indicated that the reason network viewership has declined so precipitously in the last few years is not the competition from the newer networks, video, and cable, but the extreme dissatisfaction of viewers with the lack of theocentric religion and revealed moral values represented on the networks. This same poll showed that the American people believe that prime time fiction television contributes to the destruction of the family, and that teenagers have no place else to go for entertainment. Furthermore, 45% of those interviewed indicated that they want programs that reflect explicitly Christian values. Of those polled, 70% adhered to a traditional biblical view of the family as a mother, father, and children. This poll has confused many in the entertainment industry because they are out of touch with the vast majority of the American people.

Of more concern to the entertainment industry should be the fact that many people now want the federal government to intervene to change the values presented on television. Clearly, the networks need to listen to their audiences or else these same audiences will seek to resolve the culture wars through government intervention in the entertainment industry.

There are those who feel that Americans must learn to live with religious pluralism on television. Perhaps, but the first step toward real tolerance of a multiplicity of religions on prime time entertainment television must be a concerted effort by the television executives and talent to refrain from any religious bigotry, especially the anti-Christian bigotry which is so prevalent on television today. In a study of one thousand hours of programming during the 1993 television season, the Media Research Center found that negative references to clergy outnumbered positive ones four to one. The same study found that portrayals of lay believers were even worse, with 68% of churchgoers on television depicted negatively and only 18% presented positively. Although the portrayal of clergy and churchgoers improved in 1994, the amount of anti-Christian bigotry in prime time fiction television continued to be shocking, with 31% of the clergy and 35% of the Christian laity portrayed negatively. To understand how shocking this is to Christians, imagine if 31% of the clergy of any other religion (such as Buddhist monks or Jewish rabbis) or 35% of the believers in any other religion depicted in prime time fiction television were portrayed negatively. Such bigotry would not be tolerated even though there are bad apples in every faith.

THAT GRACE MAY ABOUND

It should be noted that during the golden age of television the National Association of Broadcaster's Code prevented religious bigotry, mockery, or the defamation of people of faith on television, and perhaps as a consequence the activism of religious groups waned. Now that there is a more overt attack on revealed religions, and especially Christianity, in the mass media of entertainment, a revival of faith and activism seems to be at hand.

Throughout history persecution of the Christian faith has led to tremendous revival and growth. The persecutions of Nero, Stalin, and Mao led to an amazing growth in the number of Christian believers. In fact, the fastest way to produce Christians is to persecute them. As satirist Jonathan Swift noted, "I never saw, heard, nor read, that the clergy were beloved in any nation where Christianity was the religion of the country. Nothing can render them popular, but some degree of persecution."[16]

The magnitude of the present revival has recently been noted in the mass media in their reports on: the growth of the Christian right; growth of mega-churches; growth of nondenominational churches; and the widespread occurrence of college students throughout the United States repenting, confessing, and turning to Jesus Christ. At the same time, there has been a tremendous growth in the number of Christians taking top production positions in the entertainment industry. For example, the number-one rated television program and the biggest box office hit of 1994 were both produced by evangelical Christians. The biggest box office hit of the summer of 1995 was written by evangelical Christians. Furthermore, twenty-one of the executive producers of the sixty prime time entertainment television programs in 1994 were Christians.

Perhaps more interesting from an economic point of view is the fact that Associated Press writer George Cornell found that $56.7 billion was contributed to Christian causes in the United States in 1992, which is about 14 times the $4 billion spent on the three biggest sports: major league baseball, football, and basketball. The Gallup poll showed that a cumulative total of 5.6 billion Americans attended church in 1993, which was 55 times greater than the 103 million total attendance reported by the three main professional sports leagues. Indeed, in 1990, more Americans went to church in one month, about 430 million, than the 388 million cumulative total number of Americans who attended all sporting events during the entire year.

This rapid growth of the Christian faith may be due not only to its exclusion from and negative portrayal on much of prime time television over the last few years (although, as noted, the 1994 season showed signs of change), but also to the constant proselytizing of the anthropocentric religions which find meaning in sex, violence, and the shallow materialism of our age.

The rapid growth of the Christian faith in the midst of the culture wars has already had an impact on politics and will impact the mass media of entertainment. Of course, this revival will present new problems for those who labor in the mass media of entertainment, especially if they are bigoted and intolerant of the revealed faith of the Bible.

LIMITS

Too often in history, religions under attack, actual or imagined, have reacted in fear and aggression, and the reaction today is no different, whether in Bosnia, Northern Ireland, or Sri Lanka. Thus, tolerance on both sides should be the order of the day.

Tolerance may not bring peace to the cultural battlefield, however, because of the inherent demand and desire to proselytize built into almost every religion, and especially into Christianity, wherein Christians are called to "go and make disciples of all nations" (Matthew 28:19). Islam gives a similar command in an even more militant fashion by calling the faithful to convert or to eliminate the infidels in a jihad or holy war.

The stability of pluralism is further compromised by the fact that religion is the ultimate reality for each individual, even if that religion is atheism, humanism, or materialism. Being each man's ultimate reality, every man's religion is by definition in conflict with those who do not share the same convictions, since the various components of religion influence what each individual says, does, and expects of society.

ANSWERS

Whether or not one religious system prevails, the answer to the increasingly heated cultural wars is for the television executives and talent to be respectful of the faith of millions of Americans and for the audience to develop discernment, not denial and its companion—hate.

For the first to occur, television executives should listen to the representatives of religious groups such as our own Christian Film and Television Commission which represents a wide variety of Christians.

For the second to occur, audiences must understand the demands of drama and teach their children to discern the wheat from the chaff rather than curse the darkness. The Christian Film and Television Commission has developed a course in discernment which will help the viewer understand and use the media properly without succumbing to fear and retaliation. The course explains how to identify different religious systems and thus how to enjoy the appropriate mass media of entertainment without being unduly influenced by it.

FAITH AND GRACE

Most people do not want programs that preach at them; however, they also do not want programs that denigrate, misrepresent, or ignore their faith and undermine values that they hold dear. Rather, they want entertainment that it emotive, exciting, and worthwhile.

Tolerance does not mean that Christians and Jews need to tolerate constant attacks on their faith and values on television. Instead, it requires that the producers, executives, and talent be responsible enough to refrain from religious bigotry, as they produce programs that reflect their deeply held beliefs, even if those beliefs deny the existence of a revealed "other."

If pluralism is the order of the day, then tolerance must go along with it. The ignoring and denigrating of theocentric religions on prime time entertainment television over the last few years need to stop and the prime time schedule needs to be open to reflecting even the faith of our fathers.

NOTES

1. Ludwig Feuerbach, *The Essence of Christianity* (New York: Harper, 1957), Preface.

2. Joseph A. Schumpeter, *Capitalism, Socialism, and Democracy* (New York: Harper, 1942), Ch. 1.

3. Malcolm Muggeridge, Television broadcast, BBC1, October 21, 1965. Quoted in: Malcolm Muggeridge, "The American Way of Sex," *Muggeridge Through the Microphone* (London: British Broadcasting Corporation, 1981).

4. Camille Paglia, "Alice in Muscle Land," book review, *Boston Globe,* January 27, 1991, in *Sex, Art, and American Culture* (New York: Vintage Books, 1992).

5. E. L. Doctorow, *Billy Bathgate* (New York: Random House, 1989), Ch. 19.

6. J. M. Barrie, "The Twelve-Pound Look" (New York: Samuel French, 1914).

7. Paul Tillich, *Christianity and the Encounter of the World Religions* (New York: Columbia University Press, 1963), ch. 1.

8. Judaism, Christianity, and Islam are examples of revealed religions.

9. Certain Buddhist sects (where Buddha is recognized not as God but as an enlightened leader), Brahmanism, and Taoism are examples of non-revealed religions.

10. Henry Wadsworth Longfellow, "Meditation of Mr. Churchill, Inscribed on His Pulpit," *The Complete Poetical Works of Henry Wadsworth Longfellow* (Boston: Houghton Mifflin, 1903).

11. John Selden, "Moral Honesty," *Table Talk* (London: J. Tonson and A. J. Churchill, 1696).

12. Thirty thousand hours is slightly less than six hours a day excluding two years of infancy and incidental days away from television.

13. This figure is based on an average of eleven sexual acts and references per hour of television viewing, including commercials that are laden with sexual acts and references. Of course, the number of sexual acts and references varies depending on time of day and channel. MTV has 1,500 sexual acts and references per half-hour.

14. Eleven thousand hours assumes four hours per day of classroom time for eight months a year, excluding holidays, from ages six to seventeen. Of course, many children start in nursery school, day care, or preschool, go to after-school programs, and spend much more

than four hours per day in the classroom for more than eight months per year. Assuming six hours a day, excluding holidays, from age six to age seventeen, yields 16,000 hours.

15. Bone samples from several ancient Middle Eastern civilizations have shown that advanced cases of venereal disease may have contributed to the demise of these civilizations.

16. Jonathan Swift, "Thoughts on Religion," *Works*, 15 (London: C. Bathurst, 1765-1775).

V
Articles by
Industry Representatives

Religion, Revenue, and Ratings: Some Thoughts on Faith in Prime Time Television

Lionel Chetwynd

There is a moment in George Bernard Shaw's "Pygmalion" where Pickering demands of Doolittle, "Have you no morals, man!?" The cockney laborer ponders this for a moment then replies thoughtfully, "Can't afford them, Guv'ner." In a curious way, Doolittle could be explaining why so many television executives find the area of faith in general and religion in particular so problematic.

This is not to say that the television industry considers religious themes uncommercial; on the contrary, there is ample evidence of a large and even eager audience for the subject. The problem is, the moment one approaches the matter of religion one risks controversy—and that is a swamp that terrifies the television establishment more than the thought of riches excites them. As the common culture fractured into a multicultural mosaic (a process that dates more or less from the 1960s) mass media became the battleground for various—and at times, competing—groups to not only push for their own agenda but also to protest what they might perceive as the endorsement of a different view from their own—using op-ed invective, pressure on sponsors, and, not infrequently, demonstrations and picket lines. This is anathema to broadcasters who must, on a regular basis, reapply for the license that enables them to do business.

The result has been an urgent desire on the part of programmers to please all parties; as a consequence, such religious themes as do surface in contemporary programs are usually muted, and on the rare occasion that a religious person is depicted (positively), they are less clergymen or women than they are social workers in clerical collars.

It was not always this way; in the beginning, television was relatively unafraid of dealing—in entertainment programming—with the issues of the day. There were at least three reasons for this: (1) the cultural homogeneity of the audience; (2) the place of religion in American life; and (3) the notion of "balanced programming."

An examination of these areas, and how they have changed over television's brief lifespan, provides some sense of where we may go from here.

As already noted, there was a time when Americans seemed in general agreement on what virtues they held to be common, what values they shared, and, therefore, the general outlines of a common destiny. Interestingly, the zenith of this age was the 1950s, the same decade in which television found its place as the dominant mass medium. But the 1960s would change that atmosphere of commonality and replace it with a kind of reductionism that encouraged Americans to find the smallest group they could in order to define their public personality. One was separated first by race, then by ethnicity, then by religion (or lack of it), then by sexual orientation, and after that by a plethora of smaller and smaller subdivisions. While the idea of replacing common ground with a series of contiguous plots might be defensible (though not to this writer), it was—and is—to many people a zero-sum game. My group cannot be given proper pride of place unless your group is somehow diminished. And any praise of your views must, by definition, impoverish mine. And this argument is pressed with a grim determination fully instructed by the angry rhetoric of the sound-bite. Imagine the problems this creates for a programmer whose job depends on reaching the largest audience possible and whose business is defined—by law—as a public trust that must be regularly subjected to review by government regulatory agencies. That programmer knows instinctively that his or her job depends on avoiding controversy at all costs. And in the new national mood, religion is, per se, controversial. Which brings us to the second area of interest.

Fifty years ago, most Americans accepted religion as a commonplace feature of our national life; it was agreed that religion—whatever the denomination—was the appropriate vehicle for the transmission of the common values and ethics from one generation to another. There might be anti-papist leagues or anti-Semitic bunds, but for the vast majority of Americans, faith and religion were the source of our sense of right and wrong and, by implication, our common intercourse in the public arena. But just as the 1960s saw a shattering of our public personalities into small groups, so also was it a time when conventional wisdom about the transmission of ethical values was radically altered. The most extreme expression of this was that America was a morally flawed society and that traditional religions were the prime cause of our inhumanity. A more gentle (but with essentially the same effect) version of this was the application of postmodern deconstructionism to matters of faith. According to this argument, all belief systems are the same, even nihilism which denies any belief system whatsoever. Religion was, in this view, something of a quaint fossil to be viewed with interest but not passion. Religion, having failed in its mission of infusing ethical standards into people, was part of the problem, not the solution. This was very handy since it put the responsibility for national moral rectitude in the hands of institutions and appeared to absolve individuals of any onus for the depths into which American society was sinking. This view offered an alternative: secular humanism, the rediscovery of a personal role in shaping society. The intent was to shape a moral basis inspired not by faith—and its platform, organized religion—but by an appeal to an innate sense of right and wrong that, it was argued, was inside every human being. Secular humanism was, and is, very comfortable with multiculturalism no matter how multi it becomes. It is not my intention to pass judgment on this development (though, no doubt, my personal misgivings are clear), but simply to note it; it is the consequences that are of interest, because it was the growth of secular humanism combined with the cultural fracturing that led to a subtle but profound change in how the mass media dealt with matters of controversy, particularly when it came to issues of faith and religion.

The notion of balanced programming dominated programming decisions in the formative years of television. This idea held that if a particular view was presented in one program, it had to be balanced with a differing view by another program—and in a timely fashion. This seemed the response required by the enabling legislation from which the networks derived their licenses. Fair time and the right of response was actually spelled out in political matters and it was natural, therefore, to extend what seemed to work for politicians into general programming. It was also a practical possibility since the television schedule was dominated by dramatic anthology series: "Westinghouse Studio One," "Kraft Theater," and "Armstrong Circle Theater" were but a few of the regular programs that presented on a nightly basis what were, in effect, one act plays. It was therefore relatively simple to ensure that, for example, if a program presented a particular religious view on Monday, an alternative could be examined on Tuesday. This became much more difficult with the elimination of the single-sponsored program in favor of "spot carriers" after the payola scandals placed the blame for corruption on the vulnerability of producers being dependent on one commercial sponsor for their livelihood. Besides, the idea of the dramatic series took hold and regular characters in regular situations are, in general, less flexible in the burden of content they can bear. Hence, the notion of "balanced programming" was replaced by "balance *within* programming." The difference, though subtle, is profound. Any possibly controversial issue raised during a program had now to be answered within the same script; it was no longer acceptable to ask audiences to wait until tomorrow night to look at the question from a different point of view. The result has been a blanding of treatment of serious issues on broadcast television; we, as an audience, may be impoverished by this, but at least we are spared controversy. Religion is defined by its absence. As Kingsley Amis said of an acquaintance, "He is a Roman Catholic in the sense that this is the Church he is currently not attending."

Perhaps this was inevitable. Public Broadcasting claims to retain the old balanced programming idea and, as a result, is under constant attack from those who object to a particular presentation and lack the patience to wait until tomorrow night or next week for the balancing content of a different program.

We, as a nation, have become increasingly impatient; and, the claims of the multiculturalists notwithstanding, I believe we have become less tolerant of views other than our own. Broadcast television is market-driven, and programming reflects this.

In short, we are getting the television we deserve.

It is probably too late to change the culture of network prime time television; chances are, any improvement would make someone too uncomfortable anyway. But as the spectrum enlarges, there will ultimately be a channel for each and every religion; matters of faith will be available on demand. But they will be preaching to the converted, since I am unlikely to seek out programming that fails to speak to my own beliefs and deals with yours instead.

Faith and religion will not find their way back into mass broadcasting until we, as a nation, manage to restore civil dialogue to the public square and tolerance in the private heart.

17

Ramblings on Why Things Are the Way They Are

Bob Gale

INTRODUCTION

This article is an informal and myriad mess of ramblings, thoughts, ideas, questions, and answers which filled my head during the Religion and Prime Time Television Conference.

Who is this guy?

My name's Bob Gale. I'm a writer, producer, and director; most of my work is in motion pictures, and my best known works are the three "Back to the Future" films, which I wrote and produced. I consider myself Jewish, although I'm not a member of a congregation, nor am I terribly observant. I'm married and have a daughter, aged eight. I was born and raised in a suburb of St. Louis; my father is an attorney and my mother a musician. My politics are eclectic, but mostly right of center.

Making a career in Hollywood was my idea—it was not even on my parents' list of acceptable careers. But then, a career in show business is generally not what most parents envision for their children.

And that brings us to a question I heard raised more than once at the conference. . . .

A QUESTION

Why is it that a majority of Americans consider themselves religious and church-going, but only a minority of Hollywood professionals describe themselves as such?

A good and legitimate question to be sure. And ponder this: When it comes to describing one's religious background, the percentage of Hollywood professionals who would answer Jewish is much higher than in the general population. Why? And as long as we're asking these kinds of questions, why is the percentage of gays in show business higher than the general population?

An answer: Religion is culture. Certain professions attract people of certain cultures. And other jobs reject or are rejected by people of certain cultures.

For example, you don't see a whole lot of Jewish policemen or firemen in America. That's because: (a) these jobs are not considered as respectable in the Jewish culture as other jobs, and (b) antisemitism is a historical fact which kept Jews away from these sorts of careers. Originally these jobs were political in nature, being controlled by the Chief of Police and the Fire Chief, who were generally associated with local politicians. Jews were not part of these power structures. This holds equally with most minority groups.

If one were to take the Bible literally (and many people do), the commandment "Thou shalt not make a graven image or any likeness of anything that is in the heavens above or the earth below" pretty much rules out a career as an artist, a sculptor, or a photographer. So these are jobs where we don't find many practicing traditional Old Testament fundamentalists.

Now let's look at show business in this light. Is show business considered to be a "respectable profession" in the traditional sense of the term? Definitely not! Historically, various religions have frowned on all sorts of entertainment and public spectacle. Singing, dancing, even music have all been considered blasphemous by various sects. Dressing up in costumes and making a spectacle of oneself—what does the Bible say about that? Or the Koran? Standup comics are the historical descendants of court jesters and town fools—and that word "fool" says it all. "Running away to join the circus" is synonymous with departing legitimate society. The cardinal rule of show business is "the show must go on," and that means even on the Sabbath. Go to Career Day at any high school in America and see if you can find someone there extolling the virtues and wonderful opportunities in the world of prime time television, or rock and roll. Imagine someone coming to a religious leader for counseling: "I can't make up my mind about my career. Should I become a doctor or a teacher or an actor?" Now guess which career gets immediately eliminated.

Both culturally and historically, show business has attracted those who don't fit in, those who won't fit in, those who can't fit in, and those who aren't even allowed in. And a lot of those folks have been Jews and gays.

Given all this, it's inevitable that the people who are the most religious and devout in society are going to be among those least likely to end up in show business—it's practically by definition.

And it's therefore equally inevitable that oftentimes show biz is going to be at odds with the church.

Nowadays, things are changing. With more and more colleges and universities offering courses and degrees in television and film, the respectability factor of a career in television or film has grown tremendously. (Since they still don't teach "Circus 101," we can assume that "running away to join the circus" will continue to mean what it always has!)

And of course the awareness in society as to the power of the media (as well as the huge amounts of money the business generates) adds even more respectability.

Even the words we Hollywood folks now use to describe ourselves serve to enhance respectability. Instead of "I'm in show business," we say "I'm in the entertainment industry," "I work in broadcast media," or "I'm in the field of visual arts."

This respectability means that a career in this industry will no longer carry the stigma it once did. It means that fewer parents will automatically believe that their child's choosing a career in entertainment is equivalent to selling his/her soul. And that means that we can look to a future in which the percentage of religious, church-going members of the entertainment industry will increase.

MORE QUESTIONS

Why aren't characters on TV shows depicted as religious? Why do we so seldom see the church as an institution in the lives of TV characters?

More answers: Two answers in fact, the dramatist answer and the business answer.

The dramatist answer comes first. Drama requires conflict. A character has some sort of problem; and in the course of the drama, the problem must be solved. Example: The world's greatest heart surgeon has to perform a bypass operation. That's a problem, right? But wait; there's no drama here—we *know* that this particular surgeon can perform a bypass operation; that's what the surgeon does every day. All that this story would entail is watching the routine nuts and bolts of an expert doing his/her job, and that would be dramatically boring. For this to be an interesting story, the problem has to be serious for the character, seemingly insurmountable, and with complications. So instead of the world's greatest heart surgeon, let's make this character a small-town doctor who has never done this sort of surgery before. Now we've got a character with a serious problem. Or perhaps the patient is a murderer who killed the wife of one of the interns in the operating room. Now we've got a real conflict: the intern wants the operation to fail, the surgeon wants it to succeed. And we have the added complication of a moral dilemma for the intern: his sense of moral justice is at odds with the Hippocratic oath.

Okay, now ask yourself this: How many times have you seen a TV show and watched the characters watch television? Not very often. Think about situation comedies which take place in someone's living room. Is there a TV set there? Almost never! And yet we know that most people watch television several hours a day. Why don't TV characters watch television themselves? Because watching a character watch television is *boring*. There's no conflict. The character is passive, not active. It's about as interesting as watching someone sleep.

Similarly, watching someone attending church is boring. The sermon might be interesting, and the hymns may be beautiful, but there's no conflict, no drama. Watching a character say grace before a meal is not particularly interesting either (unless the character is, for example, a con artist who messes up the words and is in danger of being found out). So we don't put those scenes in a show unless they have a very important dramatic function.

What if we had a TV series where hero Fred Smith gets into trouble every week, prays for help, and then God answers those prayers? This might be a nice recruiting tool for the specific religion depicted, but it would be very poor drama. Why? Because Fred isn't taking action—God is. And because God can do anything, there can never be any doubt as to the outcome.

Similarly, if Fred was to ask for guidance from his pastor, get good advice, and, by taking it, solve his problem, there's not much drama here either.

The point is, the depiction of the practice of religion is not very interesting or dramatic to an audience, particularly on a week-to-week basis. And so for dramatic reasons, we generally don't depict it.

Now, there's another very powerful reason why we don't often depict religion on television—the business answer. Since there's no such thing as "generic religion," we would have to be specific about a character's particular religion. And the general public has certain preconceived notions and, yes, prejudices regarding religions. To use an extreme example, what attitude would we have about a contemporary character who worshipped the ancient Roman gods? Why, we'd ridicule this character! If we depict a Catholic, there would undoubtedly be viewers who could not identify with a Catholic, and they wouldn't watch it. And maybe the character wouldn't be as devout a Catholic as certain Catholics would like, so they'd be offended, believing that they are seeing their beliefs watered down, or even trashed. So the logical solution is to never mention a character's religion; that way, we have less chance of offending someone. We're trying to provide entertainment here, an escape. Why risk upsetting anyone?

Let's go back to the "Fred Smith Show." If Fred went to his pastor for help, got questionable advice, took it, and got himself into deeper trouble, that would be dramatic; but it would be perceived by many viewers as an anti-religious story, even though Fred is being depicted as a religious man. We'd be offending a lot of Christians, and the folks that run the networks don't want to do that. So the advice giver is changed from a pastor to a friend, or a psychiatrist, or a bartender. The networks know they won't have to worry about a national protest of bartenders.

Remember, we're not dealing with an industry full of courageous risk-taking executives. No, they want to put shows on that keep controversies to a minimum. After all, they're really in the business of selling time for commercials. Have you seen "Last Temptation of Christ" on free TV? No, and you probably never will. General Motors doesn't want to sponsor that movie, nor does Kodak or Nabisco or any major corporation, because they know a lot of people are going to be offended, and they may not buy the sponsors' products. And if the network can't sell the commercial time, they can't make a profit, and the networks are not in business to lose money. That, of course, is the bottom line: money. It's the "entertainment business," not the "entertainment nonprofit organization."

People can even be offended by things that they perceive in a show that aren't even there—things that they bring in via their own personal interpretation. Here's an example regarding "Back to the Future," a movie that I produced and co-wrote with director Robert Zemeckis. Zemeckis, who is Catholic, was told by a priest that the movie was highly offensive and delivered an insidious message, and that he had told his parishoners to avoid seeing it.

The story is a time-travel fantasy in which a boy named Marty accidentally travels back in time to the day on which his teenage parents-to-be first met. Marty accidentally gets in the middle of this, and his future mom falls in love with him instead of dad; he now has to make his future dad (who is a nerd) more attractive to mom than Marty is, otherwise Marty will never be born. In so doing, Marty makes his dad into a better person by teaching him to stand up for himself, and returns to the present to find that his dad is now a success instead of a failure. The message we intended (and which most audiences understood) is that each of us has control over his or her own destiny and that we all have the ability to take control of our lives and improve them.

Now, the movie was rated PG for some profanity and taking the name of the Lord in vain. We knew the language would offend some people, but this priest was objecting to far more than this. His view was that the movie said that if you messed up in life, you could go back to an earlier point in your life and do it over again. The priest said that this was a false promise, that man cannot interfere with God's plan, and that we must all learn to deal with our lives as they are.

Somebody will ALWAYS be offended. And if you look hard enough in your alphabet soup and keep stirring it around, you'll eventually find the letters S-A-T-A-N.

FINAL QUESTION

What will it take to get Hollywood to clean up its act?

Not an answer, but an explanation: Outsiders frequently consider "Hollywood" to be some sort of monolithic institution. Thus, we are asked questions that sound reasonable, as the above, as well as: "What is Hollywood going to do about such-and-such?" "When is Hollywood going to address this important issue?" "What does Hollywood think about this legislation?" The fact is, "Hollywood" is no more a monolithic instituition than is religion or government. When you watch the end credits of a movie or television show, look how many people are listed. And that doesn't include everyone who worked on the show! Multiply this by the number of TV shows and movies, and that will give you some idea of the huge number of people who work in "Hollywood." We are of all types, diverse in our politics, our tastes, our values, our sense of what is entertainment, our religious backgrounds, our regional backgrounds, our education, our age. Obviously, some people have more power than others to decide what shows get on the air and what movies get made. But although the studios and the networks share common ground by virtue of being the same industry, they are also competitors. They don't have some sort of shared "agenda" other than capitalism. About the only standards that everyone can get together on are union contracts and technical standards (such as color and sound levels in TV broadcasts). But artistic standards? Content standards? No way! Often, a TV show ends up on CBS because NBC rejected it. A movie gets made by Universal because it was passed on by Columbia. Production companies bid against one another for the rights to a new book. There's no conspiracy going on. There's not even any time for conspiracy, because everyone is too busy trying to make money! Tabloid television is on the air not because of some conspiracy to corrupt the public, but because people watch it and it makes money. If people didn't watch it, it would be off the air. It's the same reason that the *National Enquirer* and the *Hollywood Star* are on the newsracks. It's the same reason that there was so much media coverage of the O. J. Simpson trial: a lot of people are interested in this stuff.

Can we do better? Absolutely. Can we uplift instead of tear down? Certainly. We do so right now. Movies like "Apollo 13," "Braveheart," and "Babe" are positive, uplifiting, and fortunately, as it turns out, profitable. "ER" is quality television. And popular. So is "Home Improvement." But good and bad apples can and do grow from the same tree. You don't chop down the tree because a few bad apples grow on it. The supermarket is going to sell good food and junk food. Some people won't eat junk food, and some people eat virtually nothing but, and a lot of people indulge in some junk while eating the good stuff, too. This variety, this wide array of choices, for better and for worse, goes hand in hand with having a free, open, diverse, and capitalistic society. Not everyone is going to always like the same things—but let us thank God for that, because if we all did, things would get pretty boring.

18

A Contrariant View of Religion and TV

Danny Goldberg

Although it is entirely appropriate for religious leaders and lay people to criticize and pressure entertainment TV, from a moral point of view, there can be too much of a "good" thing.

For example, at one point during the discussion of the Religion and Prime Time Television panel of which I was a member, a young man asked me a rhetorical question which always comes up at discussions about TV entertainment and its potential for conveying moral or religious ideas or "messages." "Why," the young man asked, "would corporations spend billions of dollars on commercials to sell products, unless TV actually causes some effect on the behavior of the viewers?" This bromide comes up in virtually every debate about the effects of TV. The clear implication of the question is that commercials clearly *do* cause consumers to buy advertised products. Therefore, so goes the argument, the same medium could be used to "sell" morality. The logical extension of this point is that since TV executives and creators refrain from "selling morality," they are willfully subverting TV's moral potential, either by failing to be as astute as the questioner, or by being morally passive, or consciously consumed with profits at the expense of morality, or downright evil.

The first false premise of the young man's formulation is the assumption that the decision making process involved in weighing issues of violence or nonviolence, truth or dishonesty, selfishness or unselfishness, spiritual belief or materialism is identical to the process involved in determining which brand of toothpaste to buy, or whether or not to get a toy based on an animated action hero. In my opinion, these two categories of behavior are radically different. One involves a group of character decisions that come from the deepest core of a human being's moral universe, the other, a series of cosmically trivial decisions that have only the most transient effect on the consumer's life. It is likely that a 30-second spot might

indeed make Coke seem more "hip" than Pepsi, while a 30-minute sitcom, regardless of how well written and acted, is extremely unlikely to change the same viewer's
ideas about whether or not there is life after death.

To debunk the simplistic comparison between the peddling of products and the
peddling of moral and religious concepts is not to deny that art and entertainment
have moral and religious relevance. It is simply an attempt to move the conversation to the plane of the complex world in which real entertainers and real audiences live. There is much worth talking about in regard to problems of how religion and morality are expressed in modern mass entertainment, but the idea that
the solution is simple is not only untrue, it is dangerous.

Why dangerous? Well, if the problem of a lack of religious imagery and values
on TV is easy to solve, then it is a very short leap of logic to demonize those who
"refuse" to "fix" the "problem." A great deal of evil in the world has been caused
by demonizing people and blaming individuals or groups for eternal human problems.

There is a fairly powerful piece of evidence that religion and religious precepts
do not result so simply from some kind of enlightened brainwashing that the mere
control of a TV channel might facilitate. The Reverend Pat Robertson's organization has its own TV channel, which is in tens of millions of homes, and virtually
every home has several channels which devote hours of broadcast time to religious programming. Indeed it is virtually impossible to find anything on TV in
many parts of the United States that is mere entertainment on Sunday mornings. If
it's so easy to influence behavior with entertainment TV, why don't the religious
broadcasters, some of whom are extremely well funded, simply produce the desir-
able entertainment?

The reality is that TV entertainment, like other forms of entertainment, is driven
by entertainment values. What gets a laugh? What causes suspense? Which characters are so compelling that mass audiences will be curious enough about their
dramas to tune in week after week?

From time to time, a work of entertainment genius is created that both satisfies
a mass audience and carries a religious message. The existence of such works,
Handel's "Messiah" (or, to some of us, Spielberg's "E.T."), for example, does not
mean that all of the other entertaining but non-transcendental works were created
with a spiteful disregard for higher values. Not every ceiling can be that of the
Sistine Chapel, but that does not mean that modern ceiling painters are part of a
conspiratorial anti-religious elite.

TV is a business. If it is to be criticized as part of a comprehensive spiritual
critique of capitalism, such a critique, to be intellectually honest, must take into
account the real life spiritual and religious consequences of societies that have
adopted other systems of funding TV. The evidence is not encouraging. The BBC
is OK, but is it more moral or spiritual than ABC?

As a business TV programming is overwhelmingly driven by the desires of the
advertisers who pay the bills. Advertisers are interested primarily in certain demographic groups and uninterested in others. Thus there is almost no prime time

network TV programming about or for poor people, the elderly, non–English-speaking people, people in jail, union leaders, or many other groups representing millions of people who do not see their reality portrayed on prime time TV.

And among the tens of millions of people who are demographically favored by advertisers, there exists a genuine diversity of religious philosophy, even among those who tell pollsters they go to church on Sunday. Likewise, there exist all of the conflicts regarding questions of good and evil that religious leaders have confronted in every other arena in every other era. From this brew come tastes and predilections that TV creators, for the most part, slavishly cater to, no less than do vendors of any other kind of product vying to keep the customer satisfied.

Given this situation, all the more glory is due to visionaries such as Father Kieser, who has consistently produced spiritually uplifting entertainment within the existing TV system and whose foundation honors those in prime time TV who do likewise. But to expect a population of such visionaries available to program twenty-four hours a day, seven days a week, on several channels, is as unrealistic as expecting basketball players of the caliber of Michael Jordan to play on every high school team. God did not make the human race that way. But the human race does enjoy escapist entertainment, theologically correct or not. Moreover, no one has ever explained what's wrong with having a good non-religious laugh or cry in front of the TV set on Saturday night, and then getting religious sermons on Sunday morning.

Numerous groups have organized to try to pressure TV executives and creators, including environmentalists, feminists, gays and lesbians, and others. There is no reason whatsoever that religious groups should not follow suit to try to talk back to the community that sometimes seems to be "defining" America to itself. But the most decent and most creative people in entertainment will testify that the biggest stultifying force in entertainment is not that the powers that be at any given moment listen insufficiently to the public, but that they listen too much. They listen too much in the form of research, focus groups, and other objective barometers that keep the preponderance of mass entertainment focused on the sensibilities of the broad center of the desired audience at any given time. This business necessity creates a kind of "rearview mirror" climate for entertainment at the expense of losing the insights of true visionaries, except for those few who can combine their visions with extraordinary business and political skills.

This rearview mirror climate often results in a type of siege mentality in the entertainment community. The danger of creating such a mentality is that mediocrity and lockstep conformity to the status quo become ever more powerful and true creativity is most at risk. In this situation, the possibility of capturing and portraying true religious experience is lost as the essence of religion becomes subordinated to religious rhetoric. While it is easy to see how such repression would serve certain political agendas, it is hard to see how it would enhance traditional moral or spiritual precepts.

In the final analysis, is there any way to bring together those on different sides of this issue? I think that free speech liberals, whether religious, agnostic, or atheist, might find common cause with religious conservatives to the extent that there could be a push for increased government funding (or government mandates that TV stations themselves be required to provide funding) for TV production accountable, at least theoretically, to the entire society. We could then have future conferences about how such programming could appropriately mediate the competing demands of the diverse groups in society, including religious activists.

VI

Addendum

19

In Response to Don Wildmon

Gabriel Rossman

For the Conference on Religion and Prime Time Television, Don Wildmon eloquently decried the insufficient quantity of religion on television and the insufficiently positive nature of that little which does exist. In his speech (which is the first essay in this collection) he devoted 360 words to criticizing the "Roseanne" episode, "I Pray the Lord My Stove to Keep," ending with: "Simply put, the story is that of a young boy searching for a moral anchor. He raises the issues of lying, cheating, stealing, and illicit teen sex, and on every point his family ridicules, patronizes, or openly attacks him for implying that there aren't any standards of right and wrong in his family. Such is the state of prime time TV." The Reverend Don Wildmon feels that since the majority of the characters are cynics and act immorally, the program advocates such attitudes.

However, there is room for difference of opinion. Michael Medved (in the fourteenth selection in this volume) writes: "Over at ABC, even the 'Roseanne' show introduced a story line in which one of the main character's children began attending church regularly—and appeared to be a better person because of it." It is difficult to reconcile Medved's admiration with Wildmon's disgust. A similar view was offered by Christine Hikawa, Vice President of Broadcast Standards and Practices at ABC:

I would say this about the "Roseanne" show. . . . [W]e thought it was a brilliant examination of the absence of religion in that household. That the child could see that the mother was lying, as could we. That the child could see that the older daughter was having sex without the benefit of marriage. Our viewpoints about the outcome [of the program] may differ, but the program was an honest examination of an issue.

Everyone can agree that the "Roseanne" episode describes an immoral family. Even the characters do. When Roseanne professes an ideology of secular humanism, saying, "Basically, we believe in being good," her husband admits, "but we're not practicing." What is debatable, and debated, is whether that situation is promoted—or set up as a straw man in the underlying promotion of ethics.

Scripture itself describes immoral situations. The Bible is full of descriptions of incest, idolatry, inhospitality, murder, envy, treachery, and other immoral acts, yet it (arguably) abstains from advocating any of these despicable behaviors. Would Wildmon criticize the Bible because Lot's peers attack him for implying that there are standards of right and wrong? What about when Moses curses the Hebrews who worshipped the golden calf? Or Ezra lamenting the assimilation of the Israelites among pagans?

In all of these cases the same Biblical formula is played out; sin is ubiquitous and a believer speaks out against it. It is not the sinners, whether they be Sodomites wishing to rape angels or suburbanites embezzling stoves, who the audience is to identify with, but the outspoken believer.

Just as in the Biblical archetype the child does find a moral anchor. He finds it at church. One would assume that this would please Wildmon tremendously. After all a general decline of morality is portrayed—something that many people, religious and otherwise, perceive and decry—and faith fills the gap. This is not a story about a child of a religious family being disgusted with some form of ecclesiastical hypocrisy and fleeing the church. Rather "I Pray the Lord My Stove to Keep" is about a child disgusted with secular hypocrisy and immorality.

The only difference between "I Pray the Lord My Stove to Keep" and the Genesis story of Sodom is the lack of closure. In the typical Bible story God's side comes out on top; in "Roseanne" the situation was left unresolved. However, I think the Reverend Don Wildmon will understand the serious creative problems that would be caused by fire and brimstone falling from the heavens on the Conners' home and business, as was allegedly the case for Sodom. Likewise, a repentant Conner household, while less dramatic than annihilation of their dwelling, would break dramatically from the characters' personalities and theme of the show, which is about flawed people. The realistically moderate impact that D.J. did have, was that he kept his mother from swindling another stove and lying about his age at the movie theater. A more dramatic change, while certainly beneficial for proselytization, would ultimately make for boring television and estrange the bulk of the audience. Roseanne Arnold described the drive to avoid such a commercially undesirable situation at the Museum of Television and Radio's forum on her program: "We have to walk a real tight line when we go into shows that have some kind of depth or socially significant value to them. . . . We don't want people to start thinking about us as a preachy show, the show you watch instead of the religious channel on Sunday."

One can easily see the dilemma that television creators find themselves in. There are basically three options available to the media on religious content: preachiness, balance, and absence.

Many clergy would like to see television become "preachy," which despite the popular acclaim of the canceled program "Christy," is for the most part commercially unviable, as well as unpalatable to the secular media culture. This is because, despite what Wildmon may believe, most Americans do not believe as fervently as he does. According to the National Opinion Research Center a majority of Americans have never proselytized on behalf of Jesus. Half don't see grace said in their homes before meals. And about half of Americans only attend services several times a year or less, including the 16% who never go to church. These people can identify with "Roseanne" as they can't with "Christy," because a secular clan of suburbanites more closely reflects their values than a missionary in the Appalachian Mountains.

Alternatively television can walk the razor's edge and portray faith without proselytizing. This route was attempted by the "Roseanne" episode in question. Opinions differ as to its success in this venture. But that so many suggest failure can only frustrate the creative community. When a show attempts to portray religion in a positive (albeit humorous) light, but stops short of what Roseanne calls "preachy," it is often condemned, in what must appear a painfully arbitrary fashion to Hollywood. From this the media elite can only conclude that the safest route is to not portray religion at all.

While religious leaders may decry both a lack of religious content and a "negative" portrayal of religion, the flack garnered by the former is, by its nature, diffused. In contrast, the latter can be sharply focused into bad publicity, truckloads of mail, and boycotts. Wildmon criticized "I Pray" for its allegedly negative portrayal of religion, but he did not issue newsletters singling out the subsequent episode of "Roseanne" for its lack of religious content.

Thus it seems that religious leaders are engaged in a vicious dialectic with television. Their demands for positive portrayals of religion on mainstream television yield religion's absence from that medium by frustrating and chilling those who might attempt to present them, such as the creative talent behind "Roseanne." Ironically, it may very well be those who would most like to see religion on television who prevent its occurrence there.

Selected Bibliography

Agger, Ben. *Cultural Studies as Critical Theory*. Washington, D.C.: Falmer Press, 1992.

Anti-Defamation League. *Not the Work of a Day: The Story of the Anti-Defamation League of the B'nai B'rith*. New York: Anti-Defamation League, 1965.

Barboza, Steven. *American Jihad*. New York: Doubleday, 1993.

Barna, George. *Virtual America*. Ventura, Calif.: Regal Books, 1994.

Barnouw, Eric. *The Image Empire*. New York: Oxford University Press, 1970.

Barrie, J.M. "The Twelve-Pound Look." New York: Samuel French, 1914.

Barton, David. *The Myth of Separation*. Aledo, Tex.: WallBuilder Press, 1992.

Baudrillard, J. *In the Shadow of the Silent Majorities*. New York: Semiotext, 1983.

Bauman, Zygmunt. *Life in Fragments: Essays in Postmodern Morality*. Oxford: Blackwell Publishers, 1995.

Beahm, George, ed. *War of Words: The Censorship Debate*. Kansas City, Mo.: Andrews and McMeel, 1993.

Bedell, Kenneth B. *Yearbook of American and Canadian Churches*. Nashville, Tenn.: Abingdon Press, 1993.

_____. *Yearbook of American and Canadian Churches*. Nashville, Tenn.: Abingdon Press, 1994.

Bellah, Robert, et al. *Habits of the Heart*. Berkeley: University of California Press, 1985.

Berger, Peter. *The Sacred Canopy*. Garden City, N.Y.: Anchor, 1964.

_____. *The Heretical Imperative*. New York: Doubleday, 1980.

Bibby, Reginald. *Fragmented Gods: The Poverty and Potential of Religion in Canada*. Toronto: Irwin, 1987.

Bollinger, Lee C. *The Tolerant Society*. New York: Oxford University Press, 1986.

Bryant, Jennings, and Dolph Zillmann. *Perspectives on Media Effects*. Hillsdale, N.J.: Lawrence Erlbaum Associates, 1986.

Buchan, John. *Greenmantle*. New York: Oxford University Press, 1993.

Carter, Stephen. *The Culture of Disbelief*. New York: Doubleday, 1993.

Corbett, Michael. *Political Tolerance in America: Freedom and Equality in Public Attitudes*. New York: Longman, 1982.

Council on American-Islamic Relations. *A Rush to Judgement*. Washington, D.C.: Council on American-Islamic Relations, April 19, 1995.

Davis, Derek. "Religious Pluralism and the Quest for Unity in American Life," *Journal of Church and State* 36, Spring 1994.

Doctorow, E. L. *Billy Bathgate*. New York: Random House, 1989.

Ferre, John, ed. *Channels of Belief: Religion and American Commercial Television*. Ames: Iowa State University Press, 1990.

Feuerbach, Ludwig. *The Essence of Christianity*. New York: Harper, 1957.

Finke, Roger, and Rodney Stark. *The Churching of America, 1776-1990: Winners and Losers in Our Religious Economy*. New Brunswick, N.J.: Rutgers University Press, 1992.

Fiske, John. *Television Culture*. London: Routledge, 1987.

Fore, William F. *Television and Religion: The Shaping of Faith, Values, and Culture*. New Haven, Conn.: SBS Press, 1987.

_____. *Mythmakers: Gospel, Culture, and the Media*. New York: Friendship Press, 1990.

Gallup, George, Jr., and Frank Newport. "Americans Have Love-Hate Relationship with Their TV Sets," *The Gallup Poll Monthly*, October 1990.

Hadden, Jeffrey K. "The Rise and Fall of American Televangelism," *The Annals of the American Academy of Political and Social Science* 527, May 1993.

Hamilton, Neal F., and Alan M. Rubin. "The Influence of Religiosity on Television Viewing," *Journalism Quarterly* 69, Fall 1992.

Handy, Robert. *A Christian America: Protestant Hopes and Historical Realities*. New York: Oxford University Press, 1984.

Heins, Marjorie. *Sin, Sex, and Blasphemy: A Guide to America's Censorship Wars*. New York: The New Press, 1993.

Hoover, Stewart. "Religion in Public Discourse: The Role of the Media." Boulder, Colo.: Center for Mass Media Research, 1994.

_____. "Mass Media and Religious Pluralism," in Philip Lee, ed., *The Democratization of Communication*. Cardiff: University of Wales Press, 1996.

Hunter, James Davidson. *American Evangelicalism: Conservative Religion and the Quandary of Modernity*. New Brunswick, N.J.: Rutgers University Press, 1983.

_____. *Culture Wars: The Struggle to Define America*. New York: Basic Books, 1991.

Hunter, James Davidson, and James E. Hawdon. "Religious Elites in Advanced Capitalism: The Dialectic of Power and Marginality," in Wade Clark Roof, ed., *World Order and Religion*. Albany: SUNY Press, 1991.

Jansen, Curry. *Censorship: The Knot that Binds Power and Knowledge*. New York: Oxford University Press, 1991.

Johnson, Thomas. "Faith in a Box: Entertainment Television on Religion, 1995." Alexandria, Va.: Media Research Center, 1996.

Johnson, Thomas, and Sandra Crawford. "Faith in a Box: Entertainment Television on Religion, 1993." Alexandria, Va.: Media Research Center, 1994.

_____. "Faith in a Box: Entertainment Television on Religion, 1994." Alexandria, Va.: Media Research Center, 1995.

Keen, Sam. *Faces of the Enemy*. New York: Harper and Row, 1986.

Kellner, Douglas. "Popular Culture and the Construction of Post-Modern Identities," in Scott Lash and Jonathan Friedman, eds., *Modernity and Identity*. Oxford: Blackwell Publishers, 1992.

_____. *Media Culture: Cultural Studies, Identity, and Politics between the Modern and the Postmodern*. New York: Routledge, 1995.

Kosmin, Barry A., and Seymour P. Lachman. *One Nation Under God: Religion in Contem-*

porary American Society. New York: Harmony Books, 1993.

Lenski, Gerhard. *The Religious Factor*. Garden City, N.Y.: Doubleday, 1963.

Lichter, S. Robert, Linda Lichter, and Stanley Rothman. *Prime Time: How TV Portrays American Culture*. Washington, D.C.: Regnery Publishing, 1994.

Lindlof, Thomas R. "The Passionate Audience: Community Inscriptions of 'The Last Temptation of Christ,' " in Daniel A. Stout and Judith M. Buddenbaum, eds., *Religion and Mass Media: Audiences and Adaptations*. Thousand Oaks, Calif.: Sage, 1996.

Lippy, Charles H., and Peter W. Williams, eds. *Encyclopedia of the American Religious Experience: Studies of Traditions and Movements*. New York: Charles Scribner's Sons, 1988.

Longfellow, Henry Wadsworth. "Meditation of Mr. Churchill, Inscribed on His Pulpit," in *The Complete Poetical Works of Henry Wadsworth Longfellow*. Boston: Houghton Mifflin, 1903.

Luckman, Thomas. *The Invisible Religion*. New York: Macmillan, 1967.

Medved, Michael. *Hollywood vs. America*. New York: HarperCollins, 1992.

Melton, J. Gordon, ed. *Encyclopedic Handbook of Cults in America*. New York: Garland, 1992.

_____. *Religious Bodies in the United States: A Directory*. New York: Garland, 1992.

_____. *Encyclopedia of American Religion*. 4th ed. Washington, D.C.: Gale Research, 1993.

Michener, James. "Are There Limits to Free Speech?" in George Beahm, ed., *War of Words: The Censorship Debate*. Kansas City, Mo.: Andrews and McMeel, 1993.

Mill, John Stuart. *On Liberty*. Indianapolis, Ind.: Bobbs-Merrill, 1956.

Milton, John. "Aereopagitica," in John Patrick, ed., *The Prose of John Milton*. New York: New York University Press, 1968.

Muck, Terry. *Alien Gods on American Turf*. Wheaton, Ill.: Victor Books, 1990.

Muggeridge, Malcolm. Television broadcast, BBC1, October 21, 1965, from "The American Way of Sex," in Malcolm Muggeridge, *Muggeridge Through the Microphone*. London: British Broadcasting Corporation, 1981.

National Council of Churches. *Global Communication for Justice*. New York: National Council of Churches of Christ, 1992.

_____. "Violence in the Electronic Media," policy statement, November 11, 1993.

Noble, William. *Bookbanning in America: Who Bans Books?—and Why*. Middlebury, Vt.: Paul S. Eriksson, 1960.

Nunn, Clyde Z., Harry J. Crockett, and J. Allen Williams, Jr. *Tolerance for Nonconformity: A National Survey of Americans' Changing Commitment to Civil Liberties*. San Francisco: Jossey-Bass, 1978.

Nussbaum, Martha. *Love's Knowledge*. New York: Oxford University Press, 1990.

Oboler, E. M. *The Fear of the Word: Censorship and Sex*. Metuchen, N.J.: The Scarecrow Press, 1974.

Olasky, Marvin. *The Prodigal Press: The Anti-Christian Bias of the American News Media*. Westchester, Ill.: Crossway Books, 1988.

Paglia, Camille. "Alice in Muscle Land," in *Sex, Art, and American Culture*. New York: Vintage Books, 1992.

Parsons, Talcott. "Christianity and Modern Industrial Society," in Edward Tiryakian, ed., *Sociological Theory, Values, and Socio-Cultural Change*. New York: Free Press, 1963.

Pell, Eve. *The Big Chill: How the Reagan Administration, Corporate America, and Religious Conservatives Are Subverting Free Speech and the Public's Right to Know*. Boston: Beacon Press, 1984.

Postman, Neil. *Amusing Ourselves to Death*. New York: Penguin Books, 1985.

Protess, David L., and Maxwell McCombs, eds. *Agenda Setting: Readings on Media, Public Opinion, and Policymaking.* Hillsdale, N.J.: Lawrence Erlbaum Associates, 1991.

Richard, Alfred C. *The Hispanic Image on the Silver Screen.* Westport, Conn.: Greenwood Press, 1992.

Rimmer, Tony. "Religion, Mass Media and Tolerance for Civil Liberties," in Daniel A. Stout and Judith M. Buddenbaum, eds., *Religion and Mass Media: Audiences and Adaptations.* Thousand Oaks, Calif.: Sage, 1996.

Roberts, Churchill L. "Attitudes and Media Use of the Moral Majority," *Journal of Broadcasting* 27, Fall 1983.

Roof, Wade Clark. *A Generation of Seekers: The Spiritual Journeys of the Babyboom Generation.* San Francisco: HarperCollins, 1993.

_____, ed. *World Order and Religion.* Albany: SUNY Press, 1991.

Roof, Wade Clark, and William C. McKinney. *American Mainline Religion: Its Changing Shape and Future.* New Brunswick, N.J.: Rutgers University Press, 1987.

Schumpeter, Joseph A. *Capitalism, Socialism, and Democracy.* New York: Harper, 1942.

Selden, John. "Moral Honesty," in *Table Talk.* London: J. Tonson and A. J. Churchill, 1696.

Shaheen, Jack G. *The TV Arab.* Bowling Green, Ohio: The Popular Press, 1984.

Signorelli, Nancy, and Michael Morgan, eds. *Cultivation Analysis: New Directions in the Media Effects Research.* Newbury Park, Calif.: Sage, 1990.

Skill, Thomas, James D. Robinson, John Lyons, and David Larson. "The Portrayal of Religion and Spirituality on Fictional Network Television," *Review of Religious Research* 35, March 1994.

Skillen, James W. *The Scattered Voice: Christians at Odds in the Public Square.* Grand Rapids, Mich.: Zondervan Books, 1990.

Stokes, Anson Phelps, and Leo Pfeffer. *Church and State in the United States.* New York: Harper and Row, 1964.

Stouffer, Samuel A. *Communism, Conformity, and Civil Liberties.* Gloucester, Mass.: Peter Smith, 1963.

Stout, Daniel A., and Judith M. Buddenbaum, eds. *Religion and Mass Media: Audiences and Adaptations.* Thousand Oaks, Calif.: Sage, 1996.

Swift, Jonathan. "Thoughts on Religion," in *Works.* Vol. 15. London: C. Bathurst, 1765-1775.

Takaki, Ron. *A Different Mirror: A History of MultiCultural America.* Boston: Little, Brown, 1993.

Tillich, Paul. *Christianity and the Encounter of the World Religions.* New York: Columbia University Press, 1963.

Tussman, Joseph. *The Supreme Court on Church and State.* New York: Oxford University Press, 1962.

Valenti, JoAnn Myer, and Daniel A. Stout. "Diversity from Within: An Analysis of the Impact of Religious Culture on Media Use and Effective Communication to Women," in Daniel A. Stout and Judith M. Buddenbaum, *Religion and Mass Media: Audiences and Adaptations.* Thousand Oaks, Calif.: Sage, 1996.

Von Elton, Karen, and Tony Rimmer. "Television and Newspaper Reliance and Tolerance for Civil Liberties," *Mass Communication Review* 19, 1992.

Watterson, Bill. *Calvin and Hobbes Tenth Anniversary Book.* Kansas City, Mo.: Andrews and McMeel, 1995.

Weber, Max. "Science as a Vocation," in Hans Girth and C. Wright Mills, eds., *From Max Weber: Essays in Sociology.* New York: Oxford University Press, 1981.

Wuthnow, Robert. *The Restructuring of American Religion.* Princeton: Princeton University Press, 1988.

_____.*The Struggle for America's Soul: Evangelicals, Liberals and Secularism.* Grand Rapids, Mich.: Wm. B. Eerdmans, 1989.

Wyatt, Robert O. *Free Expression and the American Public: A Survey Commemorating the 200th Anniversary of the First Amendment.* Murfreesboro, Tenn.: Middle Tennessee State University Press, 1991.

Index

About the Editor and Contributors

Theodore Baehr is chairman of The Christian Film and Television Commission and publisher of "Movieguide," a family guide to movies and entertainment based on Judeo-Christian values. As past president of the Episcopal Radio-Television Foundation, he served as executive producer and host of the weekly PBS television program "Perspectives." Baehr has authored a number of books, including *The Christian Family Guide to Movies and Video,* Vols. 1 and 2, *Getting the Word Out*, and *Hollywood's Reel of Fortune: A Winning Strategy to Redeem the Entertainment Industry*. He received his Juris Doctor from New York University School of Law.

Dan Barker was an evangelical minister, evangelist, missionary, and Christian songwriter for nineteen years before deconverting to become an atheist. He currently works as Director of Public Relations for the Freedom From Religion Foundation in Madison, Wisconsin, a group that works to keep state and church separate and to educate the public about the views of non-theists. Dan has been a guest on many national television talk shows, including "Oprah," "Donahue," "Sally Jessy Raphael," and "Maury Povich," representing unbelief. Mr. Barker's most recent book is *Losing Faith in Faith: From Preacher to Atheist.*

Judith M. Buddenbaum is an associate professor in the Department of Journalism and Technical Communication at Colorado State University. She has worked as a religion reporter and has conducted media research for the Lutheran World Federation, Geneva, Switzerland. She is co-editor of *Religion and Mass Media: Audiences and Adaptations*. Her research on religion and the mass media has also been published in *Journalism History, Journalism Quarterly, Newspaper Research*

Journal, and as book chapters.

Joan Brown Campbell serves as the General Secretary for the National Council of the Churches of Christ in the U.S.A. She was formerly executive director of the United States Office of the World Council of Churches, and, before that, pastor at the Euclid Baptist Church, Cleveland, Ohio. Ms. Campbell received both her B.A. and M.A. from the University of Michigan and has done graduate work at both the Case Western Reserve School of Social Work and the Bossey Ecumenical Institute. She has published numerous articles on the subjects of peace, racism, women's rights, poverty, Christian unity, apartheid, the Middle East, and Christian-Jewish relations.

Lionel Chetwynd, writer, director, and producer, graduated valedictorian from Sir George University in Montreal and later attended Trinity College of Oxford University. Chetwynd wrote the motion picture screenplay adaptation for "The Apprenticeship of Duddy Kravitz," for which he received an Academy Award nomination for best screenplay adaptation. Among his other credits are the Emmy-nominated "Sadat," which received an NAACP Image Award nomination; "Miracle on Ice," which was honored with the prestigious Christopher Award; and the television movie "Johnny, We Hardly Knew Ye," for which he received the Freedom Fund's George Washington Honor Medal. Chetwynd has been a member of the faculty of New York University's Graduate Film School and has lectured on screenwriting at both the Frederick Douglass Center in Harlem and UCLA.

Archbishop **John Patrick Foley** was named President of the Pontifical Council for Social Communications, Vatican City, in 1984 by Pope John Paul II. He has chaired and served on numerous boards and commissions including the Pennsylvania State Ethics Commission, the 41st International Eucharist Congress, the National Conference of Christians and Jews, and the Catholic Press Association of the United States and Canada. He has served as editor of *The Catholic Standard*, co-produced and co-hosted the "Philadelphia Catholic Hour" on radio, and co-produced the television series "The Making of a Priest." Archbishop Foley has received the St. Francis de Sales Award from the Catholic Press Association and the Sourin Award of the Catholic Philopatrian Literacy Institute of Philadelphia. In 1991 he was made Knight Commander with Grand Cross, Order of the Northern Star, Kingdom of Sweden, and Knight Commander with Grand Cross, Order of the Holy Sepulchre.

Bob Gale, writer, director, and producer, is a USC alumnus. He wrote "Back to the Future" with Bob Zemeckis and ultimately co-produced the 1985 movie, for which he received an Academy Award nomination (with Zemeckis) for best original screenplay. Mr. Gale wrote the sequels "Back to the Future Part II" and "Part III." Gale was executive producer for the animated series "Back to the Future," which ran on CBS on Saturday mornings from 1991 to 1993. In 1991–1992, Gale co-wrote (with Zemeckis) and served as executive producer on "Trespass." In 1993, Gale wrote and directed "House of Horror" for the HBO television series "Tales from the Crypt." In 1994, Gale wrote and directed the interactive film "Mr. Payback."

Danny Goldberg, prior to being appointed President of Mercury Records, was Chairman and CEO of Warner Bros. Records and, before that, President of Atlantic Records. He also founded Gold Mountain Entertainment, a management firm whose clients included Bonnie Raitt, Nirvana, Sonic Youth, and the Beastie Boys. Beginning his career in the late 1960s, Goldberg worked as a journalist for both music trade and consumer publications, including *Billboard*, *Rolling Stone*, and *Circus*, of which he was editor. In the mid-1970s he was the U.S.-based vice president of Led Zepplin's record company Swan Song, and he went on to co-found Modern Records, as well as to supervise music on over fifteen films. He served as music consultant for the television series "Miami Vice" and co-produced and co-directed the Warner Bros. feature film "No Nukes." Goldberg has also been Chair of the American Civil Liberties Union Foundation of Southern California and currently serves as the foundation's president.

Paulist Father **Ellwood E. (Bud) Kieser**, a graduate of LaSalle University, has been working in the entertainment community in Hollywood since 1960 as a priest producer, trying to make television "a vehicle of spiritual enrichment." Kieser, ordained to the priesthood in 1956, received a Ph.D. in the theology of communications from the Graduate Theological Union in Berkeley, California. For twenty-three years Father Kieser was the executive producer of "Insight," the winner of six Emmy awards in the category of Outstanding Religious Programming. He is also President of the Human Family Institute, which awards the prestigious Humanitas Prize each year. Father Kieser is executive producer for Paulist Productions/Pictures and has produced a number of television movies, including "The Fourth Wise Man" and "We Are the Children," as well as the feature film "Romero." Kieser has also written for *Time Magazine*, the *Los Angeles Times*, *The Hollywood Reporter*, *Variety*, *America*, and *Sign*.

Michael Medved is co-host of "Sneak Previews" on PBS-TV and chief film critic for the *New York Post*. He is also the author of the controversial bestseller *Hollywood vs. America* and six other nonfiction books. His comments on media and society have appeared in the *Wall Street Journal*, *The New York Times*, *The Washington Post*, the *Boston Globe*, the *Los Angeles Times*, *Newsweek*, and many other publications, and he is a regular Hollywood correspondent for the *Sunday Times* of

London. An honors graduate of Yale, he is active in a wide variety of Jewish causes, and he was co-founder of the Pacific Jewish Center—an outreach-oriented traditional community in Venice, California.

Margaret R. Miles received her Ph.D. in history from the Graduate Theological Union at the University of California at Berkeley. Formerly Bussy Professor of Historical Theology at the Harvard University Divinity School, she is currently Dean, as well as Vice President for Academic Affairs, of the Graduate Theological Union at the University of California at Berkeley. Ms. Miles was editor for the "Religion Series" of the UMI Press, associate editor of the *Harvard Theological Review*, and co-editor of the "Harvard Dissertation Series, 1980-1990." She is the author of a number of books, including *Practicing Christianity: Critical Perspectives for an Embodied Spirituality* and the forthcoming *Seeing and Believing: Religion and Values in the Movies*.

Thomas Plate is a columnist for the *Los Angeles Times*. Before becoming a columnist, he was editor of the editorial pages for the *Los Angeles Times*, beginning in 1989. Prior to that, he served in the same capacity for *New York Newsday* and the *Los Angeles Herald Examiner*. He has also served in editorial positions for *CBS Family Weekly, Time Magazine, New York Magazine,* and *Newsday*. Mr. Plate, recipient of a master's degree from Princeton University, has held faculty positions at Santa Monica College and UCLA. He has authored a number of books including (with Andrea Darvi) *Secret Police*, a study of internal security organizations around the world. Mr. Plate has received a number of awards for his newspaper work including first place for editorials (awarded to the *Los Angeles Times*) from the California Newspaper Publishers Association in 1991, 1992, and 1994.

The Venerable **Havanpola Ratanasara**, Ph.D., in addition to being Executive President of the American Buddhist Congress, is President of the College of Buddhist Studies. He is the author of several books on Buddhism and education. He was formerly the Director of the Post-Graduate Institute of Buddhist Studies at the University of Kelaniya, Sri Lanka, and has represented Sri Lanka at the United Nations as a delegate from that country.

Wade Clark Roof, President of the Society for the Scientific Study of Religion, has been J. F. Rowny Professor of Religion and Society at the University of California, Santa Barbara, since 1989. Previously he served as Professor of Sociology at the University of Massachusetts, Amherst. He has authored or co-authored over seventy articles in professional journals and has written a number of books, including *Community and Commitment, American Mainline Religion,* and *A Genera-*

tion of Seekers. Dr. Roof's commentary has appeared in numerous periodicals, including *Time*, *Newsweek*, and *The New York Times*.

Gabriel Rossman is an intern at the UCLA Center for Communication Policy, where he works on the Center's television violence study and other projects. Rossman is currently an undergraduate majoring in sociology and communication studies at UCLA. He is assistant to the editor of the present volume.

Rabbi **A. James Rudin** is National Interreligious Affairs Director of the American Jewish Committee. He received his master's degree from the Hebrew Union College–Jewish Institute of Religion, has done graduate studies at the University of Illinois, and in 1985 was awarded an honorary Doctor of Divinity degree by HUC-JIR. A frequent contributor to op-ed pages, he also writes a weekly commentary for the New York Times Syndicate/Religious News Service and is author of many articles appearing in such prominent magazines as *Christianity Today*, *The Christian Century*, and *Commonweal*. Rabbi Rudin has authored several books, including *Israel for Christians: Understanding Modern Israel*, and has co-edited a number of others, including *Evangelicals and Jews in an Age of Pluralism*. Rudin is also a prominent social activist, involved in such activities as fighting to reform the Oberammergau play in Germany.

Jack G. Shaheen, an internationally recognized specialist on stereotypical portraits of racial and ethnic groups in mass media, is Professor Emeritus of Mass Communications at Southern Illinois University and a professional journalist. Selected by the Department of State as a Scholar-Diplomat, Dr. Shaheen lectures throughout the United States, Europe, and the Middle East. His primary focus concerns portraits of Arabs and Muslims in American popular culture. He has taught journalism at the University of Jordan and the American University of Beirut. Shaheen is a consultant with CBS News and a frequent interview subject. He has written two books, *Nuclear War Films* and *The TV Arab*. He is currently at work on *The Comic Book Arab* and *The Hollywood Arab*.

Michael Suman is Research Director of the UCLA Center for Communication Policy. He has served as project coordinator of the Center's television violence monitoring project and has co-authored several nationwide surveys. Suman, a Ph.D. in sociology from UCLA, has taught sociology, anthropology, and communication studies in Japan, Korea, China, and the Marshall Islands. He is now a member of the faculty in the Department of Communication Studies at UCLA. He is editor of the present volume.

Donald E. Wildmon, United Methodist minister and a member of the Mississippi Conference of the United Methodist Church, is also President of the American Family Association (AFA). The association works to promote Christian ethics in society with a special emphasis on the media. The monthly AFA journal has a circulation of approximately 500,000 and its broadcasting division, American Family Radio, owns and operates more than fifty FM radio stations. In addition, Wildmon is the author of twenty-two books with more than a million copies in print.

ISBN 0-275-96034-X

90000>

EAN

9 780275 960346

HARDCOVER BAR CODE